State of the Union Addresses of Rutherford B. Hayes

RUTHERFORD BIRCHARD HAYES

Published in 1877

TABLE OF CONTENTS

THE FIRST ADDRESS

State of the Union Address
Rutherford B. Hayes
December 3, 1877

Fellow-Citizens of the Senate and House of Representatives:

With devout gratitude to the bountiful Giver of All Good, I congratulate you that at the beginning of your first regular session you find our country blessed with health and peace and abundant harvests, and with encouraging prospects of an early return of general prosperity.
To complete and make permanent the pacification of the country continues to be, and until it is fully accomplished must remain, the most important of all our national interests. The earnest purpose of good citizens generally to unite their efforts in this endeavor is evident. It found decided expression in the resolutions announced in 1876 by the national conventions of the leading political parties of the country. There was a widespread apprehension that the momentous results in our progress as a nation marked by the recent amendments to the Constitution were in imminent jeopardy; that the good understanding which prompted their adoption, in the interest of a loyal devotion to the general welfare, might prove a barren truce, and that the two sections of the country, once engaged in civil strife, might be again almost as widely severed and disunited as they were when arrayed in arms against each other.
The course to be pursued, which, in my judgment, seemed wisest in the presence of this emergency, was plainly indicated in my inaugural address. It

pointed to the time, which all our people desire to see, when a genuine love of our whole country and of all that concerns its true welfare shall supplant the destructive forces of the mutual animosity of races and of sectional hostility. Opinions have differed widely as to the measures best calculated to secure this great end. This was to be expected. The measures adopted by the Administration have been subjected to severe and varied criticism. Any course whatever which might have been entered upon would certainly have encountered distrust and opposition. These measures were, in my judgment, such as were most in harmony with the Constitution and with the genius of our people, and best adapted, under all the circumstances, to attain the end in view. Beneficent results, already apparent, prove that these endeavors are not to be regarded as a mere experiment, and should sustain and encourage us in our efforts. Already, in the brief period which has elapsed, the immediate effectiveness, no less than the justice, of the course pursued is demonstrated, and I have an abiding faith that time will furnish its ample vindication in the minds of the great majority of my fellow-citizens. The discontinuance of the use of the Army for the purpose of upholding local governments in two States of the Union was no less a constitutional duty and requirement, under the circumstances existing at the time, than it was a much-needed measure for the restoration of local self-government and the promotion of national harmony. The withdrawal of the troops from such employment was effected deliberately, and with solicitous care for the peace and good order of society and the protection of the property and persons and every right of all classes of citizens.

The results that have followed are indeed significant and encouraging. All apprehension of danger from remitting those States to local self-government is dispelled, and a most salutary change in the minds of the people has begun and is in progress in every part of that section of the country once the theater of unhappy civil strife, substituting for suspicion, distrust, and aversion, concord, friendship, and patriotic attachment to the Union. No unprejudiced mind will deny that the terrible and often fatal collisions which for several years have been of frequent occurrence and have agitated and alarmed the public mind have almost entirely ceased, and that a spirit of mutual forbearance and hearty national interest has succeeded. There has been a general reestablishment of order and of the orderly administration of justice. Instances of remaining lawlessness have become of rare occurrence; political turmoil and turbulence have disappeared; useful industries have been resumed; public credit in the Southern States has been greatly strengthened, and the encouraging benefits of a revival of commerce between the sections of the country lately embroiled in civil war are fully enjoyed. Such are some of the results already attained, upon which the country is to be congratulated. They are of such importance that we may with confidence patiently await the desired consummation that will surely come with the natural progress of events.

It may not be improper here to say that it should be our fixed and unalterable determination to protect by all available and proper means under the Constitution and the laws the lately emancipated race in the enjoyment of their rights and privileges; and I urge upon those to whom heretofore the colored people have sustained the relation of bondmen the wisdom and justice of humane and liberal local legislation with respect to their education and general welfare. A firm adherence to the laws, both national and State, as to the civil and political rights of the colored people, now advanced to full and equal citizenship; the immediate repression and sure punishment by the national and local authorities, within their respective jurisdictions, of every instance of lawlessness and violence toward them, is required for the security alike of both races, and is justly demanded by the public opinion of the country and the age. In this way the restoration of harmony and good will and the complete protection of every citizen in the full enjoyment of every constitutional right will surely be attained. Whatever authority rests with me to this end I shall not hesitate to put forth.

Whatever belongs to the power of Congress and the jurisdiction of the courts of the Union, they may confidently be relied upon to provide and perform; and to the legislatures, the courts, and the executive authorities of the several States I earnestly appeal to secure, by adequate, appropriate, and seasonable means, Within their borders, these common and uniform rights of a united people which loves liberty, abhors oppression, and reveres justice. These objects are very dear to my heart. I shall continue most earnestly to strive for their attainment. The cordial cooperation of all classes, of all sections of the country and of both races, is required for this purpose; and with these blessings assured, and not otherwise, we may safely hope to hand down our free institutions of government unimpaired to the generations that will succeed us.

Among the other subjects of great and general importance to the people of this country, I can not be mistaken, I think, in regarding as preeminent the policy and measures which are designed to secure the restoration of the currency to that normal and healthful condition in which, by the resumption of specie payments, our internal trade and foreign commerce may be brought into harmony with the system of exchanges which is based upon the precious metals as the intrinsic money of the world. In the public judgment that this end should be sought and compassed as speedily and securely as the resources of the people and the wisdom of their Government can accomplish, there is a much greater degree of unanimity than is found to concur in the specific measures which will bring the country to this desired end or the rapidity of the steps by which it can be safely reached.

Upon a most anxious and deliberate examination, which I have felt it my duty to give to the subject, I am but the more confirmed in the opinion which I expressed in accepting the nomination for the Presidency, and again upon my inauguration, that the policy of resumption should be pursued by every suitable means, and that no legislation would be wise that should disparage the importance or retard the attainment of that result. I have no disposition, and certainly no right, to question the sincerity or the intelligence of opposing opinions, and would neither conceal nor undervalue the considerable difficulties, and even occasional distresses, which may attend the progress of the nation toward this primary condition to its general and permanent prosperity. I must, however, adhere to my most earnest conviction that any wavering in purpose or unsteadiness in methods, so far from avoiding or reducing the inconvenience inseparable from the transition from an irredeemable to a redeemable paper currency, would only tend to increased and prolonged disturbance in values, and unless retrieved must end in serious disorder, dishonor, and disaster in the financial affairs of the Government and of the people.

The mischiefs which I apprehend and urgently deprecate are confined to no class of the people, indeed, but seem to me most certainly to threaten the industrious masses, whether their occupations are of skilled or common labor. To them, it seems to me, it is of prime importance that their labor should be compensated in money which is itself fixed in exchangeable value by being irrevocably measured by the labor necessary to its production. This permanent quality of the money of the people is sought for, and can only be gained by the resumption of specie payments. The rich, the speculative, the operating, the money-dealing classes may not always feel the mischiefs of, or may find casual profits in, a variable currency, but the misfortunes of such a currency to those who are paid salaries or wages are inevitable and remediless.

Closely connected with this general subject of the resumption of specie payments is one of subordinate, but still of grave, importance; I mean the readjustment of our coinage system by the renewal of the silver dollar as an element in our specie currency, endowed by legislation with the quality of legal tender to a greater or less extent.

As there is no doubt of the power of Congress under the Constitution "to coin money and regulate the value thereof," and as this power covers the whole range of authority applicable to the metal, the rated value and the legal-tender quality which shall be adopted for the coinage, the considerations which should induce or discourage a particular measure connected with the coinage, belong clearly to the province of legislative discretion and of public expediency. Without intruding upon this province of legislation in the least, I have yet thought the subject of such critical importance, in the actual condition of our affairs, as to present an occasion for the exercise of the duty imposed by the Constitution on the President of recommending to the consideration of Congress "such measures as he shall judge necessary and expedient."

Holding the opinion, as I do, that neither the interests of the Government nor of the people of the United States would be promoted by disparaging silver as one of the two precious metals which furnish the coinage of the world, and that legislation which looks to maintaining the volume of intrinsic money to as full a measure of both metals as their relative commercial values will permit would be neither unjust nor inexpedient, I must ask your indulgence to a brief and definite statement of certain essential features in any such legislative measure which I feel it my duty to recommend.

I do not propose to enter the debate, represented on both sides by such able disputants in Congress and before the people and in the press, as to the extent to which the legislation of any one nation can control this question, even within its own borders, against the unwritten laws of trade or the positive laws of other governments. The wisdom of Congress in shaping any particular law that may be presented for my approval may wholly supersede the necessity of my entering into these considerations, and I willingly avoid either vague or intricate inquiries. It is only certain plain and practical traits of such legislation that I desire to recommend to your attention.

In any legislation providing for a silver coinage, regulating its value, and imparting to it the quality of legal tender, it seems to me of great importance that Congress should not lose sight of its action as operating in a twofold capacity and in two distinct directions. If the United States Government were free from a public debt, its legislative dealing with the question of silver coinage would be purely sovereign and governmental, under no restraints but those of constitutional power and the public good as affected by the proposed legislation. But in the actual circumstances of the nation, with a vast public debt distributed very widely among our own citizens and held in great amounts also abroad, the nature of the silver-coinage measure, as affecting this relation of the Government to the holders of the public debt, becomes an element, in any proposed legislation, of the highest concern. The obligation of the public faith transcends all questions of profit or public advantage otherwise. Its unquestionable maintenance is the dictate as well of the highest expediency as of the most necessary duty, and will ever be carefully guarded by Congress and people alike.

The public debt of the United States to the amount of $729,000,000 bears interest at the rate of 6 per cent, and $708,000,000 at the rate of 5 per cent, and the only way in which the country can be relieved from the payment of these high rates of interest is by advantageously refunding the indebtedness.

Whether the debt is ultimately paid in gold or in silver coin is of but little moment compared with the possible reduction of interest one-third by refunding it at such reduced rate. If the United States had the unquestioned right to pay its bonds in silver coin, the little benefit from that process would be greatly overbalanced by the injurious effect of such payment if made or proposed against the honest convictions of the public creditors.

All the bonds that have been issued since February 12, 1873, when gold became the only unlimited legal-tender metallic currency of the country, are justly payable in gold coin or in coin of equal value. During the time of these issues the only dollar that could be or was received by the Government in exchange for bonds was the gold dollar. To require the public creditors to take in repayment any dollar of less commercial value would be regarded by them as a repudiation of the full obligation assumed. The bonds issued prior to 1873 were issued at a time when the gold dollar was the only coin in circulation or contemplated by either the Government or the holders of the bonds as the coin in which they were to be paid. It is far better to pay these bonds in that coin than to seem to take advantage of the unforeseen fall in silver bullion to pay in a new issue of silver coin thus made so much less valuable. The power of the United States to coin money and to regulate the value thereof ought never to be exercised for the purpose of enabling the Government to pay its obligations in a coin of less value than that contemplated by the parties when the bonds were issued. Any attempt to pay the national indebtedness in a coinage of less commercial value than the money of the world would involve a violation of the public faith and work irreparable injury to the public credit.

It was the great merit of the act of March, 1869, in strengthening the public credit, that it removed all doubt as to the purpose of the United States to pay their bonded debt in coin. That act was accepted as a pledge of public faith. The Government has derived great benefit from it in the progress thus far made in refunding the public debt at low rates of interest. An adherence to the wise and just policy of an exact observance of the public faith will enable the Government rapidly to reduce the burden of interest on the national debt to an amount exceeding $20,000,000 per annum, and effect an aggregate saving to the United States of more than $300,000,000 before the bonds can be fully paid.

In adapting the new silver coinage to the ordinary uses of currency in the everyday transactions of life and prescribing the quality of legal tender to be assigned to it, a consideration of the first importance should be so to adjust the ratio between the silver and the gold coinage, which now constitutes our specie currency, as to accomplish the desired end of maintaining the circulation of the two metallic currencies and keeping up the volume of the two precious metals as our intrinsic money. It is a mixed question, for scientific reasoning and historical experience to determine, how far and by what methods a practical equilibrium can be maintained which will keep both metals in circulation in their appropriate spheres of common use.

An absolute equality of commercial value, free from disturbing fluctuations, is hardly attainable, and without it an unlimited legal tender for private transactions assigned to both metals would irresistibly tend to drive out of circulation the clearer coinage and disappoint the principal object proposed by the legislation in view. I apprehend, therefore, that the two conditions of a near approach to equality of commercial value between the gold and silver coinage of the same denomination and of a limitation of the amounts for which the silver coinage is to be a legal tender are essential to maintaining both in circulation. If these conditions can be successfully observed, the issue from the mint of silver dollars would afford material assistance to the community in the transition to redeemable paper money, and would facilitate the resumption of specie payment and its permanent establishment. Without these conditions I fear that only mischief and misfortune would flow from a coinage of silver dollars with the quality of unlimited legal tender, even in private transactions.

Any expectation of temporary ease from an issue of silver coinage to pass as a legal tender at a rate materially above its commercial value is, I am persuaded, a delusion. Nor can I think that there is any substantial distinction between an original issue of silver dollars at a nominal value materially above their commercial value and the restoration of the silver dollar at a rate which once was, but has ceased to be, its commercial value. Certainly the issue of our gold coinage, reduced in weight materially below its legal-tender value, would not be any the less a present debasement of the coinage by reason of its equaling, or even exceeding, in weight a gold coinage which at some past time had been commercially equal to the legal-tender value assigned to the new issue.

In recommending that the regulation of any silver coinage which may be authorized by Congress should observe these conditions of commercial value and limited legal tender, I am governed by the feeling that every possible increase should be given to the volume of metallic money which can be kept in circulation, and thereby every possible aid afforded to the people in the process of resuming specie payments. It is because of my firm conviction that a disregard of these conditions would frustrate the good results which are desired from the proposed coinage, and embarrass with new elements of confusion and uncertainty the business of the country, that I urge upon your attention these considerations.

I respectfully recommend to Congress that in any legislation providing for a silver coinage and imparting to it the quality of legal tender there be impressed upon the measure a firm provision exempting the public debt heretofore issued and now outstanding from payment, either of principal or interest, in any coinage of less commercial value than the present gold coinage of the country.

The organization of the civil service of the country has for a number of years attracted more and more of the public attention. So general has become the opinion that the methods of admission to it and the conditions of remaining in it are unsound that both the great political parties have agreed in the most explicit declarations of the necessity of reform and in the most emphatic demands for it. I have fully believed these declarations and demands to be the expression of a sincere conviction of the intelligent masses of the people upon the subject, and that they should be recognized and followed by earnest and prompt action on the part of the legislative and executive departments of the Government, in pursuance of the purpose indicated.

Before my accession to office I endeavored to have my own views distinctly understood, and upon my inauguration my accord with the public opinion was stated in terms believed to be plain and unambiguous. My experience in the executive duties has strongly confirmed the belief in the great advantage the country would find in observing strictly the plan of the Constitution, which imposes upon the Executive the sole duty and responsibility of the selection of those Federal officers who by law are appointed, not elected, and which in like manner assigns to the Senate the complete right to advise and consent to or to reject the nominations so made, whilst the House of Representatives stands as the public censor of the performance of official duties, with the prerogative of investigation and prosecution in all cases of dereliction. The blemishes and imperfections in the civil service may, as I think, be traced in most cases to a practical confusion of the duties assigned to the several Departments of the Government. My purpose in this respect has been to return to the system established by the fundamental law, and to do this with the heartiest cooperation and most cordial understanding with the Senate and House of Representatives.

The practical difficulties in the selection of numerous officers for posts of widely varying responsibilities and duties are acknowledged to be very great. No system can be expected to secure absolute freedom from mistakes, and the beginning of any attempted change of custom is quite likely to be more embarrassed in this respect than any subsequent period. It is here that the Constitution seems to me to prove its claim to the great wisdom accorded to it. It gives to the Executive the assistance of the knowledge and experience of the Senate, which, when acting upon nominations as to which they may be disinterested and impartial judges, secures as strong a guaranty of freedom from errors of importance as is perhaps possible in human affairs.

In addition to this, I recognize the public advantage of making all nominations, as nearly as possible, impersonal, in the sense of being free from mere caprice or favor in the selection; and in those offices in which special training is of greatly increased value I believe such a rule as to the tenure of office should obtain as may induce men of proper qualifications to apply themselves industriously to the task of becoming proficients. Bearing these things in mind, I have endeavored to reduce the number of changes in subordinate places usually made upon the change of the general administration, and shall most heartily cooperate with Congress in the better systematizing of such methods and rules of admission to the public service and of promotion within it as, may promise to be most successful in making thorough competency, efficiency, and character the decisive tests in these matters.

I ask the renewed attention of Congress to what has already been done by the Civil Service Commission, appointed, in pursuance of an act of Congress, by my predecessor, to prepare and revise civil-service rules. In regard to much of the departmental service, especially at Washington, it may be difficult to organize a better system than that which has thus been provided, and it is now being used to a considerable extent under my direction. The Commission has still a legal existence, although for several years no appropriation has been made for defraying its expenses. Believing that this Commission has rendered valuable service and will be a most useful agency in improving the administration of the civil service, I respectfully recommend that a suitable appropriation, to be immediately available, be made to enable it to continue its labors.

It is my purpose to transmit to Congress as early as practicable a report by the chairman of the Commission, and to ask your attention to such measures on this subject as in my opinion will further promote the improvement of the civil service.

During the past year the United States have continued to maintain peaceful relations with foreign powers.

The outbreak of war between Russia and Turkey, though at one time attended by grave apprehension as to its effect upon other European nations, has had no tendency to disturb the amicable relations existing between the United States and each of the two contending powers. An attitude of just and impartial neutrality has been preserved, and I am gratified to state that in the midst of their hostilities both the Russian and the Turkish Governments have shown an earnest disposition to adhere to the obligations of all treaties with the United States and to give due regard to the rights of American citizens.

By the terms of the treaty defining the rights, immunities, and privileges of consuls, between Italy and the United States, ratified in 1868, either Government may, after the lapse of ten years, terminate the existence of the treaty by giving twelve months' notice of its intention. The Government of Italy, availing itself of this faculty, has now given the required notice, and the treaty will accordingly end on the 17th of September, 1878. It is understood, however, that the Italian Government wishes to renew it in its general scope, desiring only certain modifications in some of its articles. In this disposition I concur, and shall hope that no serious obstacles may intervene to prevent or delay the negotiation of a satisfactory treaty.

Numerous questions in regard to passports, naturalization, and exemption from military service have continued to arise in cases of emigrants from Germany who have returned to their native country. The provisions of the treaty of February 22, 1868, however, have proved to be so ample and so judicious that the legation of the United States at Berlin has been able to adjust all claims arising under it, not only without detriment to the amicable relations existing between the two Governments, but, it is believed, without injury or injustice to any duly naturalized American citizen. It is desirable that the treaty originally made with the North German Union in 1868 should now be extended so as to apply equally to all the States of the Empire of Germany.

The invitation of the Government of France to participate in the Exposition of the Products of Agriculture, Industry, and the Fine Arts to be held at Paris during the coming year was submitted for your consideration at the extra session. It is not doubted that its acceptance by the United States, and a well-selected exhibition of the products of American industry on that occasion, will tend to stimulate international commerce and emigration, as well as to promote the traditional friendship between the two countries.

A question arose some time since as to the proper meaning of the extradition articles of the treaty of 1842 between the United States and Great Britain. Both Governments, however, are now in accord in the belief that the question is not one that should be allowed to frustrate the ends of justice or to disturb the friendship between the two nations. No serious difficulty has arisen in accomplishing the extradition of criminals when necessary. It is probable that all points of disagreement will in due time be settled, and, if need be, more explicit declarations be made in a new treaty.

The Fishery Commission under Articles XVIII to XXV of the treaty of Washington has concluded its session at Halifax. The result of the deliberations of the commission, as made public by the commissioners, will be communicated to Congress.

A treaty for the protection of trade-marks has been negotiated with Great Britain, which has been submitted to the Senate for its consideration.

The revolution which recently occurred in Mexico was followed by the accession of the successful party to power and the installation of its chief, General Porfirio Diaz, in the Presidential office. It has been the custom of the United States, when such changes of government have heretofore occurred in Mexico, to recognize and enter into official relations with the de facto government as soon as it should appear to have the approval of the

Mexican people and should manifest a disposition to adhere to the obligations of treaties and international friendship. In the present case such official recognition has been deferred by the occurrences on the Rio Grande border, the records of which have been already communicated to each House of Congress in answer to their respective resolutions of inquiry. Assurances have been received that the authorities at the seat of the Mexican Government have both the disposition and the power to prevent and punish such unlawful invasions and depredations. It is earnestly to be hoped that events may prove these assurances to be well rounded. The best interests of both countries require the maintenance of peace upon the border and the development of commerce between the two Republics.

It is gratifying to add that this temporary interruption of official relations has not prevented due attention by the representatives of the United States in Mexico to the protection of American citizens, so far as practicable; nor has it interfered with the prompt payment of the amounts due from Mexico to the United States under the treaty of July 4, 1868, and the awards of the joint commission. While I do not anticipate an interruption of friendly relations with Mexico, yet I can not but look with some solicitude upon a continuance of border disorders as exposing the two countries to initiations of popular feeling and mischances of action which are naturally unfavorable to complete amity. Firmly determined that nothing shall be wanting on my part to promote a good understanding between the two nations, I yet must ask the attention of Congress to the actual occurrences on the border, that the lives and property of our citizens may be adequately protected and peace preserved.

Another year has passed without bringing to a close the protracted contest between the Spanish Government and the insurrection in the island of Cuba. While the United States have sedulously abstained from any intervention in this contest, it is impossible not to feel that it is attended with incidents affecting the rights and interests of American citizens. Apart from the effect of the hostilities upon trade between the United States and Cuba, their progress is inevitably accompanied by complaints, having more or less foundation, of searches, arrests, embargoes, and oppressive taxes upon the property of American residents, and of unprovoked interference with American vessels and commerce. It is due to the Government of Spain to say that during the past year it has promptly disavowed and offered reparation for any unauthorized acts of unduly zealous subordinates whenever such acts have been brought to its attention. Nevertheless, such occurrences can not but tend to excite feelings of annoyance, suspicion, and resentment, which are greatly to be deprecated, between the respective subjects and citizens of two friendly powers.

Much delay (consequent upon accusations of fraud in some of the awards) has occurred in respect to the distribution of the limited amounts received from Venezuela under the treaty of April 25, 1866, applicable to the awards of the joint commission created by that treaty. So long as these matters are pending in Congress the Executive can not assume either to pass upon the questions presented or to distribute the fund received. It is eminently desirable that definite legislative action should be taken, either affirming the awards to be final or providing some method for reexamination of the claims. Our relations with the Republics of Central and South America and with the Empire of Brazil have continued without serious change, further than the temporary interruption of diplomatic intercourse with Venezuela and with Guatemala. Amicable relations have already been fully restored with Venezuela, and it is not doubted that all grounds of misunderstanding with Guatemala will speedily be removed. From all these countries there are favorable indications of a disposition on the part of their Governments and people to reciprocate our efforts in the direction of increased commercial intercourse.

The Government of the Samoan Islands has sent an envoy, in the person of its secretary of state, to invite the Government of the United States to recognize and protect their independence, to establish commercial relations with their people, and to assist them in their steps toward regulated and responsible government. The inhabitants of these islands, having made considerable progress in Christian civilization and the development of trade, are doubtful of their ability to maintain peace and independence without the aid of some stronger power. The subject is deemed worthy of respectful attention, and the claims upon our assistance by this distant community will be carefully considered.

The long commercial depression in the United States has directed attention to the subject of the possible increase of our foreign trade and the methods for its development, not only with Europe, but with other countries, and especially with the States and sovereignties of the Western Hemisphere. Instructions from the Department of State were issued to the various diplomatic and consular officers of the Government, asking them to devote attention to the question of methods by which trade between the respective countries of their official residence and the United States could be most judiciously fostered. In obedience to these instructions, examinations and reports upon this subject have been made by many of these officers and transmitted to the Department, and the same are submitted to the consideration of Congress.

The annual report of the Secretary of the Treasury on the state of the finances presents important questions for the action of Congress, upon some of which I have already remarked.

The revenues of the Government during the fiscal year ending June 30, 1877, were $269,000,586.62; the total expenditures for the same period were $238,660,008.93, leaving a surplus revenue of $30,340,577.69. This has substantially supplied the requirements of the sinking fund for that year. The estimated revenues of the current fiscal year are $265,500,000, and the estimated expenditures for the same period are $232,430,643.72. If these estimates prove to be correct, there will be a surplus revenue of $33,069,356.28—an amount nearly sufficient for the sinking fund for that year. The estimated revenues for the next fiscal year are $269,250,000. It appears from the report that during the last fiscal year the revenues of the Government, compared with the previous year, have largely decreased. This decrease, amounting to the sum of $18,481,452.54, was mainly in customs duties, caused partly by a large falling off of the amount of imported dutiable goods and partly by the general fall of prices in the markets of production of such articles as pay ad valorem taxes.

While this is felt injuriously in the diminution of the revenue, it has been accompanied with a very large increase of exportations. The total exports during the last fiscal year, including coin, have been $658,637,457, and the imports have been $492,097,540, leaving a balance of trade in favor of the United States amounting to the sum of $166,539,917, the beneficial effects of which extend to all branches of business.

The estimated revenue for the next fiscal year will impose upon Congress the duty of strictly limiting appropriations, including the requisite sum for the maintenance of the sinking fund, within the aggregate estimated receipts.

While the aggregate of taxes should not be increased, amendments might be made to the revenue laws that would, without diminishing the revenue, relieve the people from unnecessary burdens. A tax on tea and coffee is shown by the experience not only of our own country, but of other countries, to be easily collected, without loss by undervaluation or fraud, and largely borne in the country of production. A tax of 10 cents a pound on tea and 2 cents a pound on coffee would produce a revenue exceeding $12,000,000, and thus enable Congress to repeal a multitude of annoying taxes yielding a revenue not exceeding that sum. The internal-revenue system grew out of the necessities of the war, and most of the legislation imposing taxes upon domestic products under this system has been repealed. By the substitution of a tax on tea and coffee all forms of internal taxation may be repealed, except that on whisky, spirits, tobacco, and beer. Attention is also called to the necessity of enacting more vigorous laws for the protection of the revenue and for the punishment of frauds and smuggling. This can best be done by judicious provisions that will induce the disclosure of attempted fraud by undervaluation and smuggling. All revenue laws should be simple in their provisions and easily understood. So far as practicable, the rates of taxation should be in the form of specific duties, and not ad valorem, requiring the judgment of experienced men to ascertain values and exposing the revenue to the temptation of fraud.

My attention has been called during the recess of Congress to abuses existing in the collection of the customs, and strenuous efforts have been made for their correction by Executive orders. The recommendations submitted to the Secretary of the Treasury by a commission appointed to examine into the collection of customs duties at the port of New York contain many suggestions for the modification of the customs laws, to which the attention of Congress is invited.

It is matter of congratulation that notwithstanding the severe burdens caused by the war the public faith with all creditors has been preserved, and that as the result of this policy the public credit has continuously advanced and our public securities are regarded with the highest favor in the markets of the world. I trust that no act of the Government will cast a shadow upon its credit.

The progress of refunding the public debt has been rapid and satisfactory. Under the contract existing when I entered upon the discharge of the duties of my office, bonds bearing interest at the rate of 4 1/2 per cent were being rapidly sold, and within three months the aggregate sales of these bonds had reached the sum of $200,000,000. With my sanction the Secretary of the Treasury entered into a new contract for the sale of 4 per cent bonds, and within thirty days after the popular subscription for such bonds was opened subscriptions were had amounting to $75,496,550, which were paid for within ninety days after the date of subscription. By this process, within but little more than one year, the annual interest on the public debt was reduced in the sum of $3,775,000.

I recommended that suitable provision be made to enable the people to easily convert their savings into Government securities, as the best mode in which small savings may be well secured and yield a moderate interest. It is an object of public policy to retain among our own people the securities of the United States. In this way our country is guarded against their sudden return from foreign countries, caused by war or other disturbances beyond our limits.

The commerce of the United States with foreign nations, and especially the export of domestic productions, has of late years largely increased; but the greater portion of this trade is conducted in foreign vessels. The importance of enlarging our foreign trade, and especially by direct and speedy interchange with countries on this continent, can not be overestimated; and it is a matter of great moment that our own shipping interest should receive, to the utmost practical extent, the benefit of our commerce with other lands. These considerations are forcibly urged by all the large commercial cities of the country, and public attention is generally and wisely attracted to the solution of the problems they present. It is not doubted that Congress will take them up in the broadest spirit of liberality and respond to the public demand by practical legislation upon this important subject.

The report of the Secretary of War shows that the Army has been actively employed during the year, and has rendered very important service in suppressing hostilities in the Indian country and in preserving peace and protecting life and property in the interior as well as along the Mexican border. A long and arduous campaign has been prosecuted, with final complete success, against a portion of the Nez Perce tribe of Indians. A full account of this campaign will be found in the report of the General of the Army. It will be seen that in its course several severe battles were fought, in which a number of gallant officers and men lost their lives. I join with the Secretary of War and the General of the Army in awarding to the officers and men employed in the long and toilsome pursuit and in the final capture of these Indians the honor and praise which are so justly their due.

The very serious riots which occurred in several of the States in July last rendered necessary the employment of a considerable portion of the Army to preserve the peace and maintain order. In the States of West Virginia, Maryland, Pennsylvania, and Illinois these disturbances were so formidable as to defy the local and State authorities, and the National Executive was called upon, in the mode provided by the Constitution and laws, to furnish military aid. I am gratified to be able to state that the troops sent in response to these calls for aid in the suppression of domestic violence were able, by the influence of their presence in the disturbed regions, to preserve the peace and restore order without the use of force. In the discharge of this delicate and important duty both officers and men acted with great prudence and courage, and for their services deserve the thanks of the country.

Disturbances along the Rio Grande in Texas, to which I have already referred, have rendered necessary the constant employment of a military force in that vicinity. A full report of all recent military operations in that quarter has been transmitted to the House of Representatives in answer to a resolution of that body, and it will therefore not be necessary to enter into details. I regret to say that these lawless incursions into our territory by armed bands from the Mexican side of the line, for the purpose of robbery, have been of frequent occurrence, and in spite of the most vigilant efforts of the commander of our forces the marauders have generally succeeded in escaping into Mexico with their plunder. In May last I gave orders for the exercise of the utmost vigilance on the part of our troops for the suppression of these raids and the punishment of the guilty parties, as well as the recapture of property stolen by them. General Ord, commanding in Texas, was directed to invite the cooperation of the Mexican authorities in efforts to this end, and to assure them that I was anxious to avoid giving the least offense to Mexico. At the same time, he was directed to give notice of my determination to put an end to the invasion of our territory by lawless bands intent upon the plunder of our peaceful citizens, even if the effectual punishment of the outlaws should make the crossing of the border by our troops in their pursuit necessary. It is believed that this policy has had the effect to check somewhat these depredations, and that with a considerable increase of our force upon that frontier and the establishment of several additional military posts along the Rio Grande, so as more effectually to guard that extensive border, peace may be preserved and the lives and property of our citizens in Texas fully protected.

Prior to the 1st day of July last the Army was, in accordance with law, reduced to the maximum of 25,000 enlisted men, being a reduction of 2,500 below the force previously authorized. This reduction was made, as required by law, entirely from the infantry and artillery branches of the service, without any reduction of the cavalry. Under the law as it now stands it is necessary that the cavalry regiments be recruited to 100 men in each company for service on the Mexican and Indian frontiers. The necessary effect of this legislation is to reduce the infantry and artillery arms of the service below the number required for efficiency, and I concur with the Secretary of War in recommending that authority be given to recruit all companies of infantry to at least 50 men and all batteries of artillery to at least 75 men, with the power, in case of emergency, to increase the former to 100 and the latter to 122 men each.

I invite your special attention to the following recommendations of the Secretary of War:

First. That provision be made for supplying to the Army a more abundant and better supply of reading matter.

Second. That early action be taken by Congress looking to a complete revision and republication of the Army Regulations.

Third. That section 1258 of the Revised Statutes, limiting the number of officers on the retired list, be repealed.

Fourth. That the claims arising under the act of July 4, 1864, for supplies taken by the Army during the war, be taken from the offices of the Quartermaster and Commissary Generals and transferred to the Southern Claims Commission, or some other tribunal having more time and better facilities for their prompt investigation and decision than are possessed by these officers.

Fifth. That Congress provide for an annuity fund for the families of deceased soldiers, as recommended by the paymaster-General of the Army.

The report of the Secretary of the Navy shows that we have six squadrons now engaged in the protection of our foreign commerce and other duties pertaining to the naval service. The condition and operations of the Department are also shown. The total expenditures for the fiscal year ending June 30, 1877, were $16,077,974.54. There are unpaid claims against the Department chargeable to the last year, which are presented to the consideration of Congress by the report of the Secretary. The estimates for the fiscal year commencing July 1, 1878, are $16,233,234.40, exclusive of the sum of $2,314,231 submitted for new buildings, repairs, and improvements at the several navy-yards. The appropriations for the present fiscal year, commencing July 1, 1877, are $13,592,932.90. The amount drawn from the Treasury from July 1 to November 1, 1877, is $5,343,037.40, of which there is estimated to be yet available $1,029,528.30, showing the amount of actual expenditure during the first four months of the present fiscal year to have been $4,313,509.10.

The report of the Postmaster-General contains a full and clear statement of the operations and condition of the Post-Office Department. The ordinary revenues of the Department for the fiscal year ending June 30, 1877, including receipts from the money-order business and from official stamps and stamped envelopes, amounted to the sum of $27,531,585.26. The additional sum of $7,013,000 was realized from appropriations from the general Treasury for various purposes, making the receipts from all sources $34,544,885.26. The total expenditures during the fiscal year amounted to $33,486,322.44, leaving an excess of total receipts over total expenditures of $1,058,562.82, and an excess of total expenditures over ordinary receipts of $5,954,737.18. Deducting from the total receipts the sum of $63,261.84, received from international money orders of the preceding fiscal year, and deducting from the total expenditures the sum of $1,163,818.20, paid on liabilities incurred in previous fiscal years, the expenditures and receipts appertaining to the business of the last fiscal year were as follows:

Expenditures - $32,322,504.24

Receipts (ordinary, from money-order business and from official postage stamps) - 27,468,323,420 -

THE SECOND ADDRESS

State of the Union Address
Rutherford B. Hayes
December 2, 1878

Fellow-Citizens of the Senate and House of Representatives:

Our heartfelt gratitude is due to the Divine Being who holds in His hands the destinies of nations for the continued bestowal during the last year of countless blessings upon our country.

We are at peace with all other nations. Our public credit has greatly improved, and is perhaps now stronger than ever before. Abundant harvests have rewarded the labors of those who till the soil, our manufacturing industries are reviving, and it is believed that general prosperity, which has been so long anxiously looked for, is at last within our reach.

The enjoyment of health by our people generally has, however, been interrupted during the past season by the prevalence of a fatal pestilence (the yellow fever) in some portions of the Southern States, creating an emergency which called for prompt and extraordinary measures of relief. The disease appeared as an epidemic at New Orleans and at other places on the Lower Mississippi soon after midsummer. It was rapidly spread by fugitives from the infected cities and towns, and did not disappear until early in November. The States of Louisiana, Mississippi, and Tennessee have suffered severely. About 100,000 cases are believed to have occurred, of which about 20,000, according to intelligent estimates, proved fatal. It is impossible to estimate with any approach to accuracy the loss to the country occasioned by this epidemic It is to be reckoned by the hundred millions of dollars. The suffering and destitution that resulted excited the deepest sympathy in all parts of the Union. Physicians and nurses hastened from every quarter to the assistance of the afflicted communities. Voluntary contributions of money and supplies, in every needed form, were speedily and generously furnished. The Government was able to respond in some measure to the call for help, by providing tents, medicines, and food for the sick and destitute, the requisite directions for the purpose being given in the confident expectation that this action of the Executive would receive the sanction of Congress. About 1,800 tents, and rations of the value of about $25,000, were sent to cities and-towns which applied for them, full details of which will be furnished to Congress by the proper Department.

The fearful spread of this pestilence has awakened a very general public sentiment in favor of national sanitary administration, which shall not only control quarantine, but have the sanitary supervision of internal commerce in times of epidemics, and hold an advisory relation to the State and municipal health authorities, with power to deal with whatever endangers the public health, and which the municipal and State authorities are unable to regulate. The national quarantine act approved April 29, 1878, which was passed too late in the last session of Congress to provide the means for carrying it into practical operation during the past season, is a step in the direction here indicated. In view of the necessity for the most effective measures, by quarantine and otherwise, for the protection of our seaports and the country generally from this and other epidemics, it is recommended that Congress give to the whole subject early and careful consideration.

The permanent pacification of the country by the complete protection of all citizens in every civil and political right continues to be of paramount interest with the great body of our people. Every step in this direction is welcomed with public approval, and every interruption of steady and uniform progress to the desired consummation awakens general uneasiness and widespread condemnation. The recent Congressional elections have furnished a direct and trustworthy test of the advance thus far made in the practical establishment of the right of suffrage secured by the Constitution to the liberated race in the Southern States. All disturbing influences, real or imaginary, had been removed from all of these States.

The three constitutional amendments which conferred freedom and equality of civil and political rights upon the colored people of the South were adopted by the concurrent action of the great body of good citizens who maintained the authority of the National Government and the integrity and perpetuity of the Union at such a cost of treasure and life, as a wise and necessary embodiment in the organic law of the just results of the war. The people of the former slaveholding States accepted these results, and gave in every practicable form assurances that the thirteenth, fourteenth, and fifteenth amendments, and laws passed in pursuance thereof, should in good faith be enforced, rigidly and impartially, in letter and spirit, to the end that the humblest citizen, without distinction of race or color, should under them receive full and equal protection in person and property and in political rights and privileges. By these constitutional amendments the southern section of the Union obtained a large increase of political power in Congress and in the electoral college, and the country justly expected that elections would proceed, as to the enfranchised race, upon the same circumstances of legal and constitutional freedom and protection which obtained in all the other States of the Union. The friends of law and order looked forward to the conduct of these elections as offering to the general judgment of the country an important opportunity to measure the degree in which the right of suffrage could be exercised by the colored people and would be respected by their fellow-citizens; but a more general enjoyment of freedom of suffrage by the colored people and a more just and generous protection of that freedom by the communities of which they form a part were generally anticipated than the record of the elections discloses. In some of those States in which the colored people have been unable to make their opinions felt in the elections the result is mainly due to influences not easily measured or remedied by legal protection; but in the States of Louisiana and South Carolina at large, and in some particular Congressional districts outside of those States, the records of the elections seem to compel the conclusion that the rights of the colored voters have been overridden and their participation in the elections not permitted to be either general or free.

It will be for the Congress for which these elections were held to make such examinations into their conduct as may be appropriate to determine the validity of the claims of members to their seats. In the meanwhile it becomes the duty of the executive and judicial departments of the Government, each in its province, to inquire into and punish violations of the laws of the United States which have occurred. I can but repeat what I said in this connection in my last message, that whatever authority rests with me to this end I shall not hesitate to put forth; and I am unwilling to forego a renewed appeal to the legislatures, the courts, the executive authorities, and the people of the States where these wrongs have been perpetrated to give their assistance toward bringing to justice the offenders and preventing a repetition of the crimes. No means within my power will be spared to obtain a full and fair investigation of the alleged crimes and to secure the conviction and just punishment of the guilty.

It is to be observed that the principal appropriation made for the Department of Justice at the last session contained the following clause: And for defraying the expenses which may be incurred in the enforcement of the act approved February 28, 1871, entitled "An act to amend an act approved May 31, 1870, entitled 'An act to enforce the rights of citizens of the United States to vote in the several States of this Union, and for other purposes,'" or any acts amendatory thereof or supplementary thereto. It is the opinion of the Attorney-General that the expenses of these proceedings will largely exceed the amount which was thus provided, and I rely confidently upon Congress to make adequate appropriations to enable the executive department to enforce the laws.

I respectfully urge upon your attention that the Congressional elections, in every district, in a very important sense, are justly a matter of political interest and concern throughout the whole country. Each State, every political party, is entitled to the share of power which is conferred by the legal and constitutional suffrage. It is the right of every citizen possessing the qualifications prescribed by law to east one unintimidated ballot and to have his ballot honestly counted. So long as the exercise of this power and the enjoyment of this right are common and equal, practically as well as formally, submission to the results of the suffrage will be accorded loyally and cheerfully, and all the departments of Government will feel the true vigor of the popular will thus expressed. No temporary or administrative interests of Government, however urgent or weighty, will ever displace the zeal of our people in defense of the primary rights of citizenship. They understand that the protection of liberty requires the maintenance in full vigor of the manly methods of free speech, free press, and free suffrage, and will sustain the full authority of Government to enforce the laws which are framed to preserve these inestimable rights. The material progress and welfare of the States depend on the protection afforded to their citizens. There can be no peace without such protection, no prosperity without peace, and the whole country is deeply interested in the growth and prosperity of all its parts.

While the country has not yet reached complete unity of feeling and reciprocal confidence between the communities so lately and so seriously estranged, I feel an absolute assurance that the tendencies are in that direction, and with increasing force. The power of public opinion will override all political prejudices and all sectional or State attachments in demanding that all over our wide territory the name and character of citizen of the United States shall mean one and the same thing and carry with them unchallenged security and respect.

Our relations with other countries continue peaceful. Our neutrality in contests between foreign powers has been maintained and respected.

The Universal Exposition held at Paris during the past summer has been attended by large numbers of our citizens. The brief period allowed for the preparation and arrangement of the contributions of our citizens to this great exposition was well employed in energetic and judicious efforts to overcome this disadvantage. These efforts, led and directed by the commissioner-general, were remarkably successful, and the exhibition of the products of American industry was creditable and gratifying in scope and character. The reports of the United States commissioners, giving its results in detail, will be duly laid before you. Our participation in this international competition for the favor and the trade of the world may be expected to produce useful and important results—in promoting intercourse, friendship, and commerce with other nations.

In accordance with the provisions of the act of February 28, 1878, three commissioners were appointed to an international conference on the subject of adopting a common ratio between gold and silver, for the purpose of establishing internationally the use of bimetallic money and securing fixity of relative value between those metals.

Invitations were addressed to the various governments which had expressed a willingness to participate in its deliberations. The conference held its meetings in Paris in August last. The report of the commissioners, herewith submitted, will show its results. No common ratio between gold and silver could be agreed upon by the conference. The general conclusion was reached that it is necessary to maintain in the world the monetary functions of silver as well as of gold, leaving the selection of the use of one or the other of these two metals, or of both, to be made by each state.

Congress having appropriated at its last session the sum of $5,500,000 to pay the award of the joint commission at Halifax, if, after correspondence with the British Government on the subject of the conformity of the award to the requirements of the treaty and to the terms of the question thereby submitted to the commission, the President shall deem it his duty to make the payment, communications upon these points were addressed to the British Government through the legation of the United States at London. Failing to obtain the concurrence of the British Government in the views of this Government respecting the award, I have deemed it my duty to tender the sum named within the year fixed by the treaty, accompanied by a notice of the grounds of the payment and a protest against any other construction of the same. The correspondence upon this subject will be laid before you.

The Spanish Government has officially announced the termination of the insurrection in Cuba and the restoration of peace throughout that island. Confident expectations are expressed of a revival of trade and prosperity, which it is earnestly hoped may prove well rounded. Numerous claims of American citizens for relief for injuries or restoration of property have been among the incidents of the long-continued hostilities. Some of these claims are in process of adjustment by Spain, and the others are promised early and careful consideration.

The treaty made with Italy in regard to reciprocal consular privileges has been duly ratified and proclaimed.

No questions of grave importance have arisen with any other of the European powers.

The Japanese Government has been desirous of a revision of such parts of its treaties with foreign powers as relate to commerce, and it is understood has addressed to each of the treaty powers a request to open negotiations with that view. The United States Government has been inclined to regard the matter favorably. Whatever restrictions upon trade with Japan are found injurious to that people can not but affect injuriously nations holding commercial intercourse with them. Japan, after a long period of seclusion, has within the past few years made rapid strides in the path of enlightenment and progress, and, not unreasonably, is looking forward to the time when her relations with the nations of Europe and America shall be assimilated to those which they hold with each other. A treaty looking to this end has been made, which will be submitted for the consideration of the Senate.

After an interval of several years the Chinese Government has again sent envoys to the United States. They have been received, and a permanent legation is now established here by that Government. It is not doubted that this step will be of advantage to both nations in promoting friendly relations and removing causes of difference.

The treaty with the Samoan Islands, having been duly ratified and accepted on the part of both Governments, is now in operation, and a survey and soundings of the harbor of Pago-Pago have been made by a naval vessel of the United States, with a view of its occupation as a naval station if found desirable to the service.

Since the resumption of diplomatic relations with Mexico correspondence has been opened and still continues between the two Governments upon the various questions which at one time seemed to endanger their relations. While no formal agreement has been reached as to the troubles on the border, much has been done to repress and diminish them. The effective force of United States troops on the Rio Grande, by a strict and faithful compliance with instructions, has done much to remove the sources of dispute, and it is now understood that a like force of Mexican troops on the other side of the river is also making an energetic movement against the marauding Indian tribes. This Government looks with the greatest satisfaction upon every evidence of strength in the national authority of Mexico, and upon every effort put forth to prevent or to punish incursions upon our territory. Reluctant to assume any action or attitude in the control of these incursions by military movements across the border not imperatively demanded for the protection of the lives and property of our own citizens, I shall take the earliest opportunity consistent with the proper discharge of this plain duty to recognize the ability of the Mexican Government to restrain effectively violations of our territory. It is proposed to hold next year an international exhibition in Mexico, and it is believed that the display of the agricultural and manufacturing products of the two nations will tend to better understanding and increased commercial intercourse between their people.

With Brazil and the Republics of Central and South America some steps have been taken toward the development of closer commercial intercourse. Diplomatic relations have been resumed with Colombia and with Bolivia. A boundary question between the Argentine Republic and Paraguay has been submitted by those Governments for arbitration to the President of the United States, and I have, after careful examination, given a decision upon it.

A naval expedition up the Amazon and Madeira rivers has brought back information valuable both for scientific and commercial purposes. A like expedition is about visiting the coast of Africa and the Indian Ocean. The reports of diplomatic and consular officers in relation to the development of our foreign commerce have furnished many facts that have proved of public interest and have stimulated to practical exertion the enterprise of our people.

The report of the Secretary of the Treasury furnishes a detailed statement of the operations of that Department of the Government and of the condition of the public finances.

The ordinary revenues from all sources for the fiscal year ended June 30, 1878, were $257,763,878.70; the ordinary expenditures for the same period were $236,964,326.80, leaving a surplus revenue for the year of $20,799,551.90. The receipts for the present fiscal year, ending June 30, 1879, actual and estimated, are as follows: Actual receipts for the first quarter, commencing July 1, 1878, $73,389,743.43; estimated receipts for the remaining three quarters of the year, $191,110,256.57; total receipts for the current fiscal year, actual and estimated, $264,500,000. The expenditures for the same period will be, actual and estimated, as follows: For the quarter commencing July 1, 1878, actual expenditures, $73,344,573.27; and for the remaining three quarters of the year the expenditures are estimated at $166,755,426.73, making the total expenditures $240,100,000, and leaving an estimated surplus revenue for the year ending June 30, 1879, of $24,400,000. The total receipts during the next fiscal year, ending June 30, 1880, estimated according to existing laws, will be $264,500,000, and the estimated ordinary expenditures for the same period will be $236,320,412.68, leaving a surplus of $28,179,587.32 for that year.

In the foregoing statements of expenditures, actual and estimated, no amount is allowed for the sinking fund provided for by the act approved February 25, 1862, which requires that 1 per cent of the entire debt of the United States shall be purchased or paid within each fiscal year, to be set apart as a sinking fund. There has been, however, a substantial compliance with the conditions of the law. By its terms the public debt should have been reduced between 1862 and the close of the last fiscal year $518,361,806.28; the actual reduction of the ascertained debt in that period has been $720,644,739.61, being in excess of the reduction required by the sinking fund act $202,282,933.33.

The amount of the public debt, less cash in the Treasury, November 1, 1878, was $2,024,200,083.18 a reduction since the same date last year of $23,150,617.39.

The progress made during the last year in refunding the public debt at lower rates of interest is very gratifying. The amount of 4 per cent bonds sold during the present year prior to November 23, 1878, is $100,270,900, and 6 per cent bonds, commonly known as five-twenties, to an equal amount, have been or will be redeemed as calls mature.

It has been the policy of the Department to place the 4 per cent bonds within easy reach of every citizen who desires to invest his savings, whether small or great, in these securities. The Secretary of the Treasury recommends that the law be so modified that small sums may be invested, and that through the post-offices or other agents of the Government the freest opportunity may be given in all parts of the country for such investments.

The best mode suggested is that the Department be authorized to issue certificates of deposit, of the denomination of $10, bearing interest at the rate of 3.65 per cent per annum and convertible at any time within one year after their issue into the 4 per cent bonds authorized by the refunding act, and to be issued only in exchange for United States notes sent to the Treasury by mail or otherwise. Such a provision of law, supported by suitable regulations, would enable any person readily, without cost or risk, to convert his money into an interest-bearing security of the United States, and the money so received could be applied to the redemption of 6 per cent bonds.

The coinage of gold during the last fiscal year was $52,798,980. The coinage of silver dollars under the act passed February 28, 1878, amounted on the 23d of November, 1878, to $19,814,550, of which amount $4,984,947 are in circulation, and the balance, $14,829,603, is still in the possession of the Government.

With views unchanged with regard to the act under which the coinage of silver proceeds, it has been the purpose of the Secretary faithfully to execute the law and to afford a fair trial to the measure.

In the present financial condition of the country I am persuaded that the welfare of legitimate business and industry of every description will be best promoted by abstaining from all attempts to make radical changes in the existing financial legislation. Let it be understood that during the coming year the business of the country will be undisturbed by governmental interference with the laws affecting it, and we may confidently expect that the resumption of specie payments, which will take place at the appointed time, will be successfully and easily maintained, and that it will be followed by a healthful and enduring revival of business prosperity.

Let the healing influence of time, the inherent energies of our people, and the boundless resources of our country have a fair opportunity, and relief from present difficulties will surely follow.

The report of the Secretary of War shows that the Army has been well and economically supplied; that our small force has been actively employed and has faithfully performed all the service required of it. The morale of the Army has improved and the number of desertions has materially decreased during the year.

The Secretary recommends—

1. That a pension be granted to the widow of the late Lieutenant Henry H. Benner, Eighteenth Infantry, who lost his life by yellow fever while in command of the steamer. J.M. Chambers, sent with supplies for the relief of sufferers in the South from that disease.

2. The establishment of the annuity scheme for the benefit of the heirs of deceased officers, as suggested by the Paymaster-General.

3. The adoption by Congress of a plan for the publication of the records of the War of the Rebellion, now being prepared for that purpose.

4. The increase of the extra per diem of soldier teachers employed in post schools, and liberal appropriations for the erection of buildings for schools and libraries at the different posts.

5. The repeal or amendment of the act of June 18, 1878, forbidding the use of the Army "as a posse comitatus, or otherwise, for the purpose of executing the laws, except in such cases and under such circumstances as such employment of said force may be expressly authorized by the Constitution or by act of Congress."

6. The passage of a joint resolution of Congress legalizing the issues of rations, tents, and medicines which were made for the relief of sufferers from yellow fever.

7. That provision be made for the erection of a fireproof building for the preservation of certain valuable records, now constantly exposed to destruction by fire.

These recommendations are all commended to your favorable consideration.

The report of the Secretary of the Navy shows that the Navy has improved during the last fiscal year. Work has been done on seventy-five vessels, ten of which have been thoroughly repaired and made ready for sea. Two others are in rapid progress toward completion. The total expenditures of the year, including the amount appropriated for the deficiencies of the previous year, were $17,468,392.65. The actual expenses chargeable to the year, exclusive of these deficiencies, were $13,306,914.09, or $767,199.18 less than those of the previous year, and $4,928,677.74 less than the expenses including the deficiencies. The estimates for the fiscal year ending

June 30, 1880, are $14,562,381.45, exceeding the appropriations of the present year only $33,949.75, which excess is occasioned by the demands of the Naval Academy and the Marine Corps, as explained in the Secretary's report. The appropriations for the present fiscal year are $14,528,431.70, which, in the opinion of the Secretary, will be ample for all the current expenses of the Department during the year. The amount drawn from the Treasury from July 1 to November 1, 1878, is $4,740,544.14, of which $70,980.75 has been refunded, leaving as the expenditure for that period $4,669,563.39, or $520,899.24 less than the corresponding period of the last fiscal year.

The report of the Postmaster-General embraces a detailed statement of the operations of the Post-Office Department. The expenditures of that Department for the fiscal year ended June 30, 1878, were $34,165,084.49. The receipts, including sales of stamps, money-order business, and official stamps, were $29,277,516.95. The sum of $290,436.90, included in the foregoing statement of expenditures, is chargeable to preceding years, so that the actual expenditures for the fiscal year ended June 30, 1878, are $33,874,647.59. The amount drawn from the Treasury on appropriations, in addition to the revenues of the Department, was $5,307,652.82. The expenditures for the fiscal year ending June 30, 1880, are estimated at $36,571,900 and the receipts from all sources at $30,664,023.90, leaving a deficiency to be appropriated out of the Treasury of $5,907,876.10. The report calls attention to the fact that the compensation of postmasters and of railroads for carrying the mail is regulated by law, and that the failure of Congress to appropriate the amounts required for these purposes does not relieve the Government of responsibility, but necessarily increases the deficiency bills which Congress will be called upon to pass.

In providing for the postal service the following questions are presented: Should Congress annually appropriate a sum for its expenses largely in excess of its revenues, or should such rates of postage be established as will make the Department self-sustaining? Should the postal service be reduced by excluding from the mails matter which does not pay its way? Should the number of post routes be diminished? Should other methods be adopted which will increase the revenues or diminish the expenses of the postal service?

The International Postal Congress which met at Paris May 1, 1878, and continued in session until June 4 of the same year, was composed of delegates from nearly all the civilized countries of the world. It adopted a new convention (to take the place of the treaty concluded at Berne October 9, 1874), which goes into effect on the 1st of April, 1879, between the countries whose delegates have signed it. It was ratified and approved, by and with the consent of the President, August 13, 1878. A synopsis of this Universal Postal Convention will be found in the report of the Postmaster-

General, and the full text in the appendix thereto. In its origin the Postal Union comprised twenty-three countries, having a population of 350,000,000 people. On the 1st of April next it will comprise forty-three countries and colonies, with a population of more than 650,000,000 people, and will soon, by the accession of the few remaining countries and colonies which maintain organized postal services, constitute in fact as well as in name, as its new title indicates, a universal union, regulating, upon a uniform basis of cheap postage rates, the postal intercourse between all civilized nations.

Some embarrassment has arisen out of the conflict between the customs laws of this country and the provisions of the Postal Convention in regard to the transmission of foreign books and newspapers to this country by mail. It is hoped that Congress will be able to devise some means of reconciling the difficulties which have thus been created, so as to do justice to all parties involved.

The business of the Supreme Court and of the courts in many of the circuits has increased to such an extent during the past year that additional legislation is imperative to relieve and prevent the delay of justice and possible oppression to suitors which is thus occasioned. The encumbered condition of these dockets is presented anew in the report of the Attorney-General, and the remedy suggested is earnestly urged for Congressional action. The creation of additional circuit judges, as proposed, would afford a complete remedy, and would involve an expense, at the present rate of salaries of not more than $60,000 a year.

The annual reports of the Secretary of the Interior and of the Commissioner of Indian Affairs present an elaborate account of the present condition of the Indian tribes and of that branch of the public service which ministers to their interests. While the conduct of the Indians generally has been orderly and their relations with their neighbors friendly and peaceable, two local disturbances have occurred, which were deplorable in their character, but remained, happily, confined to a comparatively small number of Indians. The discontent among the Bannocks, which led first to some acts of violence on the part of some members of the tribe and finally to the outbreak, appears to have been caused by an insufficiency of food on the reservation, and this insufficiency to have been owing to the inadequacy of the appropriations made by Congress to the wants of the Indians at a time when the Indians were prevented from supplying the deficiency by hunting. After an arduous pursuit by the troops of the United States, and several engagements, the hostile Indians were reduced to subjection, and the larger part of them surrendered themselves as prisoners. In this connection I desire to call attention to the recommendation made by the Secretary of the Interior, that a sufficient fund be placed at the disposal of the Executive, to be used, with proper accountability, at discretion, in sudden emergencies of the Indian service.

The other case of disturbance was that of a band of Northern Cheyennes, who suddenly left their reservation in the Indian Territory and marched rapidly through the States of Kansas and Nebraska in the direction of their old hunting grounds, committing murders and other crimes on their way. From documents accompanying the report of the Secretary of the Interior it appears that this disorderly band was as fully supplied with the necessaries of life as the 4,700 other Indians who remained quietly on the reservation, and that the disturbance was caused by men of a restless and mischievous disposition among the Indians themselves. Almost the whole of this band have surrendered to the military authorities; and it is a gratifying fact that when some of them had taken refuge in the camp of the Red Cloud Sioux, with whom they had been in friendly relations, the Sioux held them as prisoners and readily gave them up to the officers of the United States, thus giving new proof of the loyal spirit which, alarming rumors to the contrary notwithstanding, they have uniformly shown ever since the wishes they expressed at the council of September, 1877, had been complied with.

Both the Secretary of the Interior and the Secretary of War unite in the recommendation that provision be made by Congress for the organization of a corps of mounted "Indian auxiliaries," to be under the control of the Army and to be used for the purpose of keeping the Indians on their reservations and preventing or repressing disturbance on their part. I earnestly concur in this recommendation. It is believed that the organization of such a body of Indian cavalry, receiving a moderate pay from the Government, would considerably weaken the restless element among the Indians by withdrawing from it a number of young men and giving them congenial employment under the Government, it being a matter of experience that Indians in our service almost without exception are faithful in the performance of the duties assigned to them. Such an organization would materially aid the Army in the accomplishment of a task for which its numerical strength is sometimes found insufficient.

But while the employment of force for the prevention or repression of Indian troubles is of occasional necessity, and wise preparation should be made to that end, greater reliance must be placed on humane and civilizing agencies for the ultimate solution of what is called the Indian problem. It may be very difficult and require much patient effort to curb the unruly spirit of the savage Indian to the restraints of civilized life, but experience shows that it is not impossible. Many of the tribes which are now quiet and orderly and self-supporting were once as savage as any that at present roam over the plains or in the mountains of the far West, and were then considered inaccessible to civilizing influences. It may be impossible to raise them fully up to the level of the white population of the United States; but we should not forget that they are the aborigines of the country, and called the soil their own on which our people have grown rich, powerful, and happy. We owe it to them as a moral duty to help them in attaining at least that degree of civilization which they may be able to reach. It is not only our duty, it is also our interest to do so. Indians who have become agriculturists or herdsmen, and feel an interest in property, will thenceforth cease to be a warlike and disturbing element. It is also a well-authenticated fact that Indians are apt to be peaceable and quiet when their children are at school, and I am gratified to know, from the expressions of Indians themselves and from many concurring reports, that there is a steadily increasing desire, even among Indians belonging to comparatively wild tribes, to have their children educated. I invite attention to the reports of the Secretary of the Interior and the Commissioner of Indian Affairs touching the experiment recently inaugurated, in taking fifty Indian children, boys and girls, from different tribes, to the Hampton Normal Agricultural Institute in Virginia, where they are to receive an elementary English education and training in agriculture and other useful works, to be returned to their tribes, after the completed course, as interpreters, instructors, and examples. It is reported that the officer charged with the selection of those children might have had thousands of young Indians sent with him had it been possible to make provision for them. I agree with the Secretary of the Interior in saying that "the result of this interesting experiment, if favorable, may be destined to become an important factor in the advancement of civilization among the Indians."

The question whether a change in the control of the Indian service should be made was at the last session of Congress referred to a committee for inquiry and report. Without desiring to anticipate that report, I venture to express the hope that in the decision of so important a question the views expressed above may not be lost sight of, and that the decision, whatever it may be, will arrest further agitation of this subject, such agitation being apt to produce a disturbing effect upon the service, as well as on the Indians themselves.

In the enrollment of the bill making appropriations for sundry civil expenses, at the last session of Congress, that portion which provided for the continuation of the Hot Springs Commission was omitted. As the commission had completed the work of taking testimony on the many conflicting claims, the suspension of their labors, before determining the rights of claimants, threatened for a time to embarrass the interests, not only of the Government, but also of a large number of the citizens of Hot Springs, who were waiting for final action on their claims before beginning contemplated improvements. In order to prevent serious difficulties, which were apprehended, and at the solicitation of many leading citizens of Hot Springs and others interested in the welfare of the town, the Secretary of the Interior was authorized to request the late commissioners to take charge of the records of their proceedings and to perform such work as could properly be done by them under such circumstances to facilitate the future adjudication of the claims at an early day and to preserve the status of the claimants until their rights should be finally determined. The late commissioners complied with that request, and report that the testimony in all the cases has been written out, examined, briefed, and so arranged as to facilitate an early settlement when authorized by law. It is recommended that the requisite authority be given at as early a day in the session as possible, and that a fair compensation be allowed the late commissioners for the expense incurred and the labor performed by them since the 25th of June last.

I invite the attention of Congress to the recommendations made by the Secretary of the Interior with regard to the preservation of the timber on the public lands of the United States. The protection of the public property is one of the first duties of the Government. The Department of the Interior should therefore be enabled by sufficient appropriations to enforce the laws in that respect. But this matter appears still more important as a question of public economy. The rapid destruction of our forests is an evil fraught with the gravest consequences, especially in the mountainous districts, where the rocky slopes, once denuded of their trees, will remain so forever. There the injury, once done, can not be repaired. I fully concur with the Secretary of the Interior in the opinion that for this reason legislation touching the public timber in the mountainous States and Territories of the West should be especially well considered, and that existing laws in which the destruction of the forests is not sufficiently guarded against should be speedily modified. A general law concerning this important subject appears to me to be a matter of urgent public necessity.

From the organization of the Government the importance of encouraging by all possible means the increase of our agricultural productions has been acknowledged and urged upon the attention of Congress and the people as the surest and readiest means of increasing our substantial and enduring prosperity.

The words of Washington are as applicable to-day as when, in his eighth annual message, he said: It will not be doubted that, with reference either to individual or national welfare, agriculture is of primary importance. In proportion as nations advance in population and other circumstances of maturity this truth becomes more apparent, and renders the cultivation of the soil more and more an object of public patronage. Institutions for promoting it grow up, supported by the public purse; and to what object can it be dedicated with greater propriety? Among the means which have been employed to this end none have been attended with greater success than the establishment of boards (composed of proper characters) charged with collecting and diffusing information, and enabled by premiums and small pecuniary aids to encourage and assist a spirit of discovery and improvement. This species of establishment contributes doubly to the increase of improvement, by stimulating to enterprise and experiment, and by drawing to a common center the results everywhere of individual skill and observation and spreading them thence over the whole nation. Experience accordingly hath shewn that they are very cheap instruments of immense national benefits. The preponderance of the agricultural over any other interest in the United States entitles it to all the consideration claimed for it by Washington. About one-half of the population of the United States is engaged in agriculture. The value of the agricultural products of the United States for the year 1878 is estimated at $3,000,000,000. The exports of agricultural products for the year 1877, as appears from the report of the Bureau of Statistics, were $524,000,000. The great extent of our country, with its diversity of soil and climate, enables us to produce within our own borders and by our own labor not only the necessaries, but most of the luxuries, that are consumed in civilized countries. Yet, notwithstanding our advantages of soil, climate, and inter-communication, it appears from the statistical statements in the report of the Commissioner of Agriculture that we import annually from foreign lands many millions of dollars worth of agricultural products which could be raised in our own country.

Numerous questions arise in the practice of advanced agriculture which can only be answered by experiments, often costly and sometimes fruitless, which are beyond the means of private individuals and are a just and proper charge on the whole nation for the benefit of the nation. It is good policy, especially in times of depression and uncertainty in other business pursuits, with a vast area of uncultivated, and hence unproductive, territory, wisely opened to homestead settlement, to encourage by every proper and legitimate means the occupation and tillage of the soil. The efforts of the Department of Agriculture to stimulate old and introduce new agricultural industries, to improve the quality and increase the quantity of our products, to determine the value of old or establish the importance of new methods of culture, are worthy of your careful and favorable consideration, and assistance by such appropriations of money and enlargement of facilities as may seem to be demanded by the present favorable conditions for the growth and rapid development of this important interest.

The abuse of animals in transit is widely attracting public attention. A national convention of societies specially interested in the subject has recently met at Baltimore, and the facts developed, both in regard to cruelties to animals and the effect of such cruelties upon the public health, would seem to demand the careful consideration of Congress and the enactment of more efficient laws for the prevention of these abuses.

The report of the Commissioner of the Bureau of Education shows very gratifying progress throughout the country in all the interests committed to the care of this important office. The report is especially encouraging with respect to the extension of the advantages of the common-school system in sections of the country where the general enjoyment of the privilege of free schools is not yet attained.

To education more than to any other agency we are to look as the resource for the advancement of the people in the requisite knowledge and appreciation of their rights and responsibilities as citizens, and I desire to repeat the suggestion contained in my former message in behalf of the enactment of appropriate measures by Congress for the purpose of supplementing with national aid the local systems of education in the several States.

Adequate accommodations for the great library, which is overgrowing the capacity of the rooms now occupied at the Capitol, should be provided without further delay. This invaluable collection of books, manuscripts, and illustrative art has grown to such proportions, in connection with the copyright system of the country, as to demand the prompt and careful attention of Congress to save it from injury in its present crowded and insufficient quarters. As this library is national in its character, and must from the nature of the case increase even more rapidly in the future than in the past, it can not be doubted that the people will sanction any wise expenditure to preserve it and to enlarge its usefulness.

The appeal of the Regents of the Smithsonian Institution for the means to organize, exhibit, and make available for the public benefit the articles now stored away belonging to the National Museum I heartily recommend to your favorable consideration.

The attention of Congress is again invited to the condition of the river front of the city of Washington. It is a matter of vital importance to the health of the residents of the national capital, both temporary and permanent, that the lowlands in front of the city, now subject to tidal overflow, should be reclaimed. In their present condition these flats obstruct the drainage of the city and are a dangerous source of malarial poison. The reclamation will improve the navigation of the river by restricting, and consequently deepening, its channel, and is also of importance when considered in connection with the extension of the public ground and the enlargement of the park west and south of the Washington Monument. The report of the board of survey, heretofore ordered by act of Congress, on the improvement of the harbor of Washington and Georgetown, is respectfully commended to consideration.

The report of the Commissioners of the District of Columbia presents a detailed statement of the affairs of the District.

The relative expenditures by the United States and the District for local purposes is contrasted, showing that the expenditures by the people of the District greatly exceed those of the General Government. The exhibit is made in connection with estimates for the requisite repair of the defective pavements and sewers of the city, which is a work of immediate necessity; and in the same connection a plan is presented for the permanent funding of the outstanding securities of the District.

The benevolent, reformatory, and penal institutions of the District are all entitled to the favorable attention of Congress. The Reform School needs additional buildings and teachers. Appropriations which will place all of these institutions in a condition to become models of usefulness and beneficence will be regarded by the country as liberality wisely bestowed.

The Commissioners, with evident justice, request attention to the discrimination made by Congress against the District in the donation of land for the support of the public schools, and ask that the same liberality that has been shown to the inhabitants of the various States and Territories of the United States may be extended to the District of Columbia.

The Commissioners also invite attention to the damage inflicted upon public and private interests by the present location of the depots and switching tracks of the several railroads entering the city, and ask for legislation looking to their removal. The recommendations and suggestions contained in the report will, I trust, receive the careful consideration of Congress.

Sufficient time has, perhaps, not elapsed since the reorganization of the government of the District under the recent legislation of Congress for the expression of a confident opinion as to its successful operation, but the practical results already attained are so satisfactory that the friends of the new government may well urge upon Congress the wisdom of its continuance, without essential modification, until by actual experience its advantages and defects may be more fully ascertained.

R. B. HAYES

THE THIRD ADDRESS

State of the Union Address
Rutherford B. Hayes
December 1, 1879

Fellow-Citizens of the Senate and House of Representatives:

The members of the Forty-sixth Congress have assembled in their first regular session under circumstances calling for mutual congratulation and grateful acknowledgment to the Giver of All Good for the large and unusual measure of national prosperity which we now enjoy.

The most interesting events which have occurred in our public affairs since my last annual message to Congress are connected with the financial operations of the Government, directly affecting the business interests of the country. I congratulate Congress on the successful execution of the resumption act. At the time fixed, and in the manner contemplated by law, United States notes began to be redeemed in coin. Since the 1st of January last they have been promptly redeemed on presentation, and in all business transactions, public and private, in all parts of the country, they are received and paid out as the equivalent of coin. The demand upon the Treasury for gold and silver in exchange for United States notes has been comparatively small, and the voluntary deposit of coin and bullion in exchange for notes has been very large. The excess of the precious metals deposited or exchanged for United States notes over the amount of United States notes redeemed is about $40,000,000.

The resumption of specie payments has been followed by a very great revival of business. With a currency equivalent in value to the money of the commercial world, we are enabled to enter upon an equal competition with other nations in trade and production. The increasing foreign demand for our manufactures and agricultural products has caused a large balance of trade in our favor, which has been paid in gold, from the 1st of July last to November 15, to the amount of about $59,000,000. Since the resumption of specie payments there has also been a marked and gratifying improvement of the public credit. The bonds of the Government bearing only 4 per cent interest have been sold at or above par, sufficient in amount to pay off all of the national debt which was redeemable under present laws. The amount of interest saved annually by the process of refunding the debt since March 1, 1877, is $14,297,177. The bonds sold were largely in small sums, and the number of our citizens now holding the public securities is much greater than ever before. The amount of the national debt which matures within less than two years is $792,121,700, of which $500,000,000 bear interest at the rate of 5 per cent, and the balance is in bonds bearing 6 per cent interest. It is believed that this part of the public debt can be refunded by the issue of 4 per cent bonds, and, by the reduction of interest which will thus be effected, about $11,000,000 can be annually saved to the Treasury. To secure this important reduction of interest to be paid by the United States further legislation is required, which it is hoped will be provided by Congress during its present session.

The coinage of gold by the mints of the United States during the last fiscal year was $40,986,912. The coinage of silver dollars since the passage of the act for that purpose up to November 1, 1879, was $45,000,850, of which $12,700,344 have been issued from the Treasury and are now in circulation, and $32,300,506 are still in the possession of the Government.

The pendency of the proposition for unity of action between the United States and the principal commercial nations of Europe to effect a permanent system for the equality of gold and silver in the recognized money of the world leads me to recommend that Congress refrain from new legislation on the general subject. The great revival of trade, internal and foreign, will supply during the coming year its own instructions, which may well be awaited before attempting further experimental measures with the coinage. I would, however, strongly urge upon Congress the importance of authorizing the Secretary of the Treasury to suspend the coinage of silver dollars upon the present legal ratio. The market value of the silver dollar being uniformly and largely less than the market value of the gold dollar, it is obviously impracticable to maintain them at par with each other if both are coined without limit. If the cheaper coin is forced into circulation, it will, if coined without limit, soon become the sole standard of value, and thus defeat the desired object, which is a currency of both gold and silver which shall be of equivalent value, dollar for dollar, with the universally recognized money of the world.

The retirement from circulation of United States notes with the capacity of legal tender in private contracts is a step to be taken in our progress toward a safe and stable currency which should be accepted as the policy and duty of the Government and the interest and security of the people. It is my firm conviction that the issue of legal-tender paper money based wholly upon the authority and credit of the Government, except in extreme emergency, is without warrant in the Constitution and a violation of sound financial principles. The issue of United States notes during the late civil war with the capacity of legal tender between private individuals was not authorized except as a means of rescuing the country from imminent peril. The circulation of these notes as paper money for any protracted period of time after the accomplishment of this purpose was not contemplated by the framers of the law under which they were issued. They anticipated the redemption and withdrawal of these notes at the earliest practicable period consistent with the attainment of the object for which they were provided.

The policy of the United States, steadily adhered to from the adoption of the Constitution, has been to avoid the creation of a national debt; and when, from necessity in time of war, debts have been created, they have been paid off, on the return of peace, as rapidly as possible. With this view, and for this purpose, it is recommended that the existing laws for the accumulation of a sinking fund sufficient to extinguish the public debt within a limited period be maintained. If any change of the objects or rates of taxation is deemed necessary by Congress, it is suggested that experience has shown that a duty can be placed on tea and coffee which will not enhance the price of those articles to the consumer, and which will add several millions of dollars annually to the Treasury.

The continued deliberate violation by a large number of the prominent and influential citizens of the Territory of Utah of the laws of the United States for the prosecution and punishment of polygamy demands the attention of every department of the Government. This Territory has a population sufficient to entitle it to admission as a State, and the general interests of the nation, as well as the welfare of the citizens of the Territory, require its advance from the Territorial form of government to the responsibilities and privileges of a State. This important change will not, however, be approved by the country while the citizens of Utah in very considerable number uphold a practice which is condemned as a crime by the laws of all civilized communities throughout the world.

The law for the suppression of this offense was enacted with great unanimity by Congress more than seventeen years ago, but has remained until recently a dead letter in the Territory of Utah, because of the peculiar difficulties attending its enforcement. The opinion widely prevailed among the citizens of Utah that the law was in contravention of the constitutional guaranty of religious freedom. This objection is now removed. The Supreme Court of the United States has decided the law to be within the legislative power of Congress and binding as a rule of action for all who reside within the Territories. There is no longer any reason for delay or hesitation in its enforcement. It should be firmly and effectively executed. If not sufficiently stringent in its provisions, it should be amended; and in aid of the purpose in view I recommend that more comprehensive and more searching methods for preventing as well as punishing this crime be provided. If necessary to secure obedience to the law, the enjoyment and exercise of the rights and privileges of citizenship in the Territories of the United States may be withheld or withdrawn from those who violate or oppose the enforcement of the law on this subject.

The elections of the past year, though occupied only with State officers, have not failed to elicit in the political discussions which attended them all over the country new and decisive evidence of the deep interest which the great body of citizens take in the progress of the country toward a more general and complete establishment, at whatever cost, of universal security and freedom in the exercise of the elective franchise. While many topics of political concern demand great attention from our people, both in the sphere of national and State authority, I find no reason to qualify the opinion I expressed in my last annual message, that no temporary or administrative interests of government, however urgent or weighty, will ever displace the zeal of our people in defense of the primary rights of citizenship, and that the power of public opinion will override all political prejudices, and all sectional and State attachments in demanding that all over our wide territory the name and character of citizen of the United States shall mean one and the same thing and carry with them unchallenged security and respect. I earnestly appeal to the intelligence and patriotism of all good citizens of every part of the country, however much they maybe divided in opinions on other political subjects, to unite in compelling obedience to existing laws aimed at the protection of the right of suffrage. I respectfully urge upon Congress to supply any defects in these laws which experience has shown and which it is within its power to remedy. I again invoke the cooperation of the executive and legislative authorities of the States in this great purpose. I am fully convinced that if the public mind can be set at rest on this paramount question of popular rights no serious obstacle will thwart or delay the complete pacification of the country or retard the general diffusion of prosperity.

In a former message I invited the attention of Congress to the subject of the reformation of the civil service of the Government, and expressed the intention of transmitting to Congress as early as practicable a report upon this subject by the chairman of the Civil Service Commission.

In view of the facts that during a considerable period the Government of Great Britain has been dealing with administrative problems and abuses in various particulars analogous to those presented in this country, and that in recent years the measures adopted were understood to have been effective and in every respect highly satisfactory, I thought it desirable to have fuller information upon the subject, and accordingly requested the chairman of the Civil Service Commission to make a thorough investigation for this purpose. The result has been an elaborate and comprehensive report.

The report sets forth the history of the partisan spoils system in Great Britain, and of the rise and fall of the parliamentary patronage, and of official interference with the freedom of elections. It shows that after long trials of various kinds of examinations those which are competitive and open on equal terms to all, and which are carried on under the superintendence of a single commission, have, with great advantage, been established as conditions of admission to almost every official place in the subordinate administration of that country and of British India. The completion of the report, owing to the extent of the labor involved in its preparation and the omission of Congress to make any provision either for the compensation or the expenses of the Commission, has been postponed until the present time. It is herewith transmitted to Congress.

While the reform measures of another government are of no authority for us, they are entitled to influence to the extent to which their intrinsic wisdom and their adaptation to our institutions and social life may commend them to our consideration. The views I have heretofore expressed concerning the defects and abuses in our civil administration remain unchanged, except in so far as an enlarged experience has deepened my sense of the duty both of officers and of the people themselves to cooperate for their removal. The grave evils and perils of a partisan spoils system of appointment to office and of office tenure are now generally recognized. In the resolutions of the great parties, in the reports of Departments, in the debates and proceedings of Congress, in the messages of Executives, the gravity of these evils has been pointed out and the need of their reform has been admitted.

To command the necessary support, every measure of reform must be based on common right and justice, and must be compatible with the healthy existence of great parties, which are inevitable and essential in a free state.

When the people have approved a policy at a national election, confidence on the part of the officers they have selected and of the advisers who, in accordance with our political institutions, should be consulted in the policy which it is their duty to carry into effect is indispensable. It is eminently proper that they should explain it before the people, as well as illustrate its spirit in the performance of their official duties.

Very different considerations apply to the greater number of those who fill the subordinate places in the civil service. Their responsibility is to their superiors in official position. It is their duty to obey the legal instructions of those upon whom that authority is devolved, and their best public service consists in the discharge of their functions irrespective of partisan politics. Their duties are the same whatever party is in power and whatever policy prevails. As a consequence it follows that their tenure of office should not depend on the prevalence of any policy or the supremacy of any party, but should be determined by their capacity to serve the people most usefully quite irrespective of partisan interests. The same considerations that should govern the tenure should also prevail in the appointment, discipline, and removal of these subordinates. The authority of appointment and removal is not a perquisite, which may be used to aid a friend or reward a partisan, but is a trust, to be exercised in the public interest under all the sanctions which attend the obligation to apply the public funds only for public purposes.

Every citizen has an equal right to the honor and profit of entering the public service of his country. The only just ground of discrimination is the measure of character and capacity he has to make that service most useful to the people. Except in cases where, upon just and recognized principles— as upon the theory of pensions—offices and promotions are bestowed as rewards for past services, their bestowal upon any theory which disregards personal merit is an act of injustice to the citizen, as well as a breach of that trust subject to which the appointing power is held.

In the light of these principles it becomes of great importance to provide just and adequate means, especially for every Department and large administrative office, where personal discrimination on the part of its head is not practicable, for ascertaining those qualifications to which appointments and removals should have reference. To fail to provide such means is not only to deny the opportunity of ascertaining the facts upon which the most righteous claim to office depends, but of necessity to discourage all worthy aspirants by handing over appointments and removals to mere influence and favoritism. If it is the right of the worthiest claimant to gain the appointment and the interest of the people to bestow it upon him, it would seem clear that a wise and just method of ascertaining personal fitness for office must be an important and permanent function of every just and wise government. It has long since become impossible in the great offices for those having the duty of nomination and appointment to personally examine into the individual qualifications of more than a small proportion of those seeking office, and with the enlargement of the civil service that proportion must continue to become less.

In the earlier years of the Government the subordinate offices were so few in number that it was quite easy for those making appointments and promotions to personally ascertain the merits of candidates. Party managers and methods had not then become powerful agencies of coercion, hostile to the free and just exercise of the appointing power.

A large and responsible part of the duty of restoring the civil service to the desired purity and efficiency rests upon the President, and it is my purpose to do what is within my power to advance such prudent and gradual measures of reform as will most surely and rapidly bring about that radical change of system essential to make our administrative methods satisfactory to a free and intelligent people. By a proper exercise of authority it is in the power of the Executive to do much to promote such a reform. But it can not be too clearly understood that nothing adequate can be accomplished without cooperation on the part of Congress and considerate and intelligent support among the people. Reforms which challenge the generally accepted theories of parties and demand changes in the methods of Departments are not the work of a day. Their permanent foundations must be laid in sound principles and in an experience which demonstrates their wisdom and exposes the errors of their adversaries. Every worthy officer desires to make his official action a gain and an honor to his country; but the people themselves, far more than their officers in public station, are interested in a pure, economical, and vigorous administration.

By laws enacted in 1853 and 1855, and now in substance incorporated in the Revised Statutes, the practice of arbitrary appointments to the several subordinate grades in the great Departments was condemned, and examinations as to capacity, to be conducted by departmental boards of examiners, were provided for and made conditions of admission to the public service. These statutes are a decision by Congress that examinations of some sort as to attainments and capacity are essential to the well-being of the public service. The important questions since the enactment of these laws have been as to the character of these examinations, and whether official favor and partisan influence or common right and merit were to control the access to the examinations. In practice these examinations have not always been open to worthy persons generally who might wish to be examined. Official favoritism and partisan influence, as a rule, appear to have designated those who alone were permitted to go before the examining boards, subjecting even the examiners to a pressure from the friends of the candidates very difficult to resist. As a consequence the standard of admission fell below that which the public interest demanded. It was also almost inevitable that a system which provided for various separate boards of examiners, with no common supervision or uniform method of procedure, should result in confusion, inconsistency, and inadequate tests of capacity, highly detrimental to the public interest. A further and more radical change was obviously required.

In the annual message of December, 1870, my predecessor declared that—
There is no duty which so much embarrasses the Executive and heads of Departments as that of appointments, nor is there any such arduous and thankless labor imposed on Senators and Representatives as that of finding

places for constituents. The present system does not secure the best men, and often not even fit men, for public place. The elevation and purification of the civil service of the Government will be hailed with approval by the whole people of the United States. Congress accordingly passed the act approved March 3, 1871, "to regulate the civil service of the United States and promote the efficiency thereof," giving the necessary authority to the Executive to inaugurate a civil-service reform.

Acting under this statute, which was interpreted as intended to secure a system of just and effectual examinations under uniform supervision, a number of eminently competent persons were selected for the purpose, who entered with zeal upon the discharge of their duties, prepared with an intelligent appreciation of the requirements of the service the regulations contemplated, and took charge of the examinations, and who in their capacity as a board have been known as the "Civil Service Commission." Congress for two years appropriated the money needed for the compensation and for the expense of carrying on the work of the Commission.

It appears from the report of the Commission submitted to the President in April, 1874, that examinations had been held in various sections of the country, and that an appropriation of about $25,000 would be required to meet the annual expenses, including salaries, involved in discharging the duties of the Commission. The report was transmitted to Congress by special message of April 18, 1874, with the following favorable comment upon the labors of the Commission: If sustained by Congress, I have no doubt the rules can, after the experience gained, be so improved and enforced as to still more materially benefit the public service and relieve the Executive, members of Congress, and the heads of Departments from influences prejudicial to good administration. The rules, as they have hitherto been enforced, have resulted beneficially, as is shown by the opinions of the members of the Cabinet and their subordinates in the Departments, and in that opinion I concur. And in the annual message of December of the same year similar views are expressed and an appropriation for continuing the work of the Commission again advised.

The appropriation was not made, and as a consequence the active work of the Commission was suspended, leaving the Commission itself still in existence. Without the means, therefore, of causing qualifications to be tested in any systematic manner or of securing for the public service the advantages of competition upon any extensive plan, I recommended in my annual message of December, 1877, the making of an appropriation for the resumption of the work of the Commission.

In the meantime, however, competitive examinations, under many embarrassments, have been conducted within limited spheres in the Executive Departments in Washington and in a number of the custom-houses and post-offices of the principal cities of the country, with a view to further test their effects, and in every instance they have been found to be as salutary as they are stated to have been under the Administration of my predecessor. I think the economy, purity, and efficiency of the public service would be greatly promoted by their systematic introduction, wherever practicable, throughout the entire civil service of the Government, together with ample provision for their general supervision in order to secure consistency and uniform justice.

Reports from the Secretary of the Interior, from the Postmaster-General, from the postmaster in the city of New York, where such examinations have been some time on trial, and also from the collector of the port, the naval officer, and the surveyor in that city, and from the postmasters and collectors in several of the other large cities, show that the competitive system, where applied, has in various ways contributed to improve the public service.

The reports show that the results have been salutary in a marked degree, and that the general application of similar rules can not fail to be of decided benefit to the service.

The reports of the Government officers, in the city of New York especially, bear decided testimony to the utility of open competitive examinations in their respective offices, showing that—These examinations and the excellent qualifications of those admitted to the service through them have had a marked incidental effect upon the persons previously in the service, and particularly upon those aspiring to promotion. There has been on the part of these latter an increased interest in the work and a desire to extend acquaintance with it beyond the particular desk occupied, and thus the morale of the entire force has been raised. The examinations have been attended by many citizens, who have had an opportunity to thoroughly investigate the scope and character of the tests and the method of determining the results, and those visitors have without exception approved the methods employed, and several of them have publicly attested their favorable opinion. Upon such considerations I deem it my duty to renew the recommendation contained in my annual message of December, 1877, requesting Congress to make the necessary appropriation for the resumption of the work of the Civil Service Commission. Economy will be promoted by authorizing a moderate compensation to persons in the public service who may perform extra labor upon or under the Commission, as the Executive may direct.

I am convinced that if a just and adequate test of merit is enforced for admission to the public service and in making promotions such abuses as removals without good cause and partisan and official interference with the proper exercise of the appointing power will in large measure disappear.

There are other administrative abuses to which the attention of Congress should be asked in this connection. Mere partisan appointments and the constant peril of removal without cause very naturally lead to an absorbing and mischievous political activity on the part of those thus appointed, which not only interferes with the due discharge of official duty, but is incompatible with the freedom of elections. Not without warrant in the views of several of my predecessors in the Presidential office, and directly within the law of 1871, already cited, I endeavored, by regulation made on the 22d day of June, 1877, to put some reasonable limits to such abuses. It may not be easy, and it may never perhaps be necessary, to define with precision the proper limit of political action on the part of Federal officers. But while their right to hold and freely express their opinions can not be questioned, it is very plain that they should neither be allowed to devote to other subjects the time needed for the proper discharge of their official duties nor to use the authority of their office to enforce their own opinions or to coerce the political action of those who hold different opinions.

Reasons of justice and public policy quite analogous to those which forbid the use of official power for the oppression of the private citizen impose upon the Government the duty of protecting its officers and agents from arbitrary exactions. In whatever aspect considered, the practice of making levies for party purposes upon the salaries of officers is highly demoralizing to the public service and discreditable to the country. Though an officer should be as free as any other citizen to give his own money in aid of his opinions or his party, he should also be as free as any other citizen to refuse to make such gifts. If salaries are but a fair compensation for the time and labor of the officer, it is gross injustice to levy a tax upon them. If they are made excessive in order that they may bear the tax, the excess is an indirect robbery of the public funds.

I recommend, therefore, such a revision and extension of present statutes as shall secure to those in every grade of official life or public employment the protection with which a great and enlightened nation should guard those who are faithful in its service.

Our relations with foreign countries have continued peaceful.

With Great Britain there are still unsettled questions, growing out of the local laws of the maritime provinces and the action of provincial authorities deemed to be in derogation of rights secured by treaty to American fishermen. The United States minister in London has been instructed to present a demand for $105,305.02 in view of the damages received by American citizens at Fortune Bay on the 6th day of January, 1878. The subject has been taken into consideration by the British Government, and an early reply is anticipated.

Upon the completion of the necessary preliminary examinations the subject of our participation in the provincial fisheries, as regulated by treaty, will at once be brought to the attention of the British Government, with a view to an early and permanent settlement of the whole question, which was only temporarily adjusted by the treaty of Washington.

Efforts have been made to obtain the removal of restrictions found injurious to the exportation of cattle to the United Kingdom.

Some correspondence has also occurred with regard to the rescue and saving of life and property upon the Lakes, which has resulted in important modifications of the previous regulations of the Dominion government on the subject in the interest of humanity and commerce.

In accordance with the joint resolution of the last session of Congress, commissioners were appointed to represent the United States at the two international exhibitions in Australia, one of which is now in progress at Sydney, and the other to be held next year at Melbourne. A desire has been expressed by our merchants and manufacturers interested in the important and growing trade with Australia that an increased provision should be made by Congress for the representation of our industries at the Melbourne exhibition of next year, and the subject is respectfully submitted to your favorable consideration.

The assent of the Government has been given to the landing on the coast of Massachusetts of a new and independent transatlantic cable between France, by way of the French island of St. Pierre, and this country, subject to any future legislation of Congress on the subject. The conditions imposed before allowing this connection with our shores to be established are such as to secure its competition with any existing or future lines of marine cable and preclude amalgamation therewith, to provide for entire equality of rights to our Government and people with those of France in the use of the cable, and prevent any exclusive possession of the privilege as accorded by France to the disadvantage of any future cable communication between France and the United States which may be projected and accomplished by our citizens. An important reduction of the present rates of cable communication with Europe, felt to be too burdensome to the interests of our commerce, must necessarily flow from the establishment of this competing line.

The attention of Congress was drawn to the propriety of some general regulation by Congress of the whole subject of transmarine cables by my predecessor in his message of December 7, 1875, and I respectfully submit to your consideration the importance of Congressional action in the matter.

The questions of grave importance with Spain growing out of the incidents of the Cuban insurrection have been for the most part happily and honorably settled. It may reasonably be anticipated that the commission now sitting in Washington for the decision of private cases in this connection will soon be able to bring its labors to a conclusion.

The long-standing question of East Florida claims has lately been renewed as a subject of correspondence, and may possibly require Congressional action for its final disposition.

A treaty with the Netherlands with respect to consular rights and privileges similar to those with other powers has been signed and ratified, and the ratifications were exchanged on the 31st of July last. Negotiations for extradition treaties with the Netherlands and with Denmark are now in progress.

Some questions with Switzerland in regard to pauper and convict emigrants have arisen, but it is not doubted that they will be arranged upon a just and satisfactory basis. A question has also occurred with respect to an asserted claim by Swiss municipal authorities to exercise tutelage over persons and property of Swiss citizens naturalized in this country. It is possible this may require adjustment by treaty.

With the German Empire frequent questions arise in connection with the Subjects of naturalization and expatriation, but the Imperial Government has constantly manifested a desire to strictly maintain and comply with all treaty stipulations in regard to them.

In consequence of the omission of Congress to provide for a diplomatic representative at Athens, the legation to Greece has been withdrawn. There is now no channel of diplomatic communication between the two countries, and the expediency of providing for one in some form is submitted to Congress.

Relations with Austria, Russia, Italy, Portugal, Turkey, and Belgium continue amicable, and marked by no incident of especial importance.

A change of the personal head of the Government of Egypt has taken place. No change, however, has occurred in the relations between Egypt and the United States. The action of the Egyptian Government in presenting to the city of New York one of the ancient obelisks, which possess such historic interest, is highly appreciated as a generous mark of international regard. If prosperity should attend the enterprise of its transportation across the Atlantic, its erection in a conspicuous position in the chief commercial city of the nation will soon be accomplished.

The treaty recently made between Japan and the United States in regard to the revision of former commercial treaties it is now believed will be followed by similar action on the part of other treaty powers. The attention of Congress is again invited to the subject of the indemnity funds received some years since from Japan and China, which, with their accumulated interest, now amount to considerable sums. If any part of these funds is justly due to American citizens, they should receive it promptly; and whatever may have been received by this Government in excess of strictly just demands should in some form be returned to the nations to whom it equitably belongs.

The Government of China has signified its willingness to consider the question of the emigration of its subjects to the United States with a dispassionate fairness and to cooperate in such measures as may tend to prevent injurious consequences to the United States. The negotiations are still proceeding, and will be pressed with diligence.

A question having arisen between China and Japan about the Lew Chew Islands, the United States Government has taken measures to inform those powers of its readiness to extend its good offices for the maintenance of peace if they shall mutually deem it desirable and find it practicable to avail themselves of the proffer.

It is a gratification to be able to announce that, through the judicious and energetic action of the military commanders of the two nations on each side of the Rio Grande, under the instructions of their respective Governments, raids and depredations have greatly decreased, and in the localities where formerly most destructive have now almost wholly ceased. In view of this result, I entertain a confident expectation that the prevalence of quiet on the border will soon become so assured as to justify a modification of the present orders to our military commanders as to crossing the border, without encouraging such disturbances as would endanger the peace of the two countries.

The third installment of the award against Mexico under the claims commission of July 4, 1868, was duly paid, and has been put in course of distribution in pursuance of the act of Congress providing for the same. This satisfactory situation between the two countries leads me to anticipate an expansion of our trade with Mexico and an increased contribution of capital and industry by our people to the development of the great resources of that country. I earnestly commend to the wisdom of Congress the provision of suitable legislation looking to this result.

Diplomatic intercourse with Colombia is again fully restored by the arrival of a minister from that country to the United States. This is especially fortunate in view of the fact that the question of an inter-oceanic canal has recently assumed a new and important aspect and is now under discussion with the Central American countries through whose territory the canal, by the Nicaragua route, would have to pass. It is trusted that enlightened statesmanship on their part will see that the early prosecution of such a work will largely inure to the benefit, not only of their own citizens and those of the United States, but of the commerce of the civilized world. It is not doubted that should the work be undertaken under the protective auspices of the United States, and upon satisfactory concessions for the right of way and its security by the Central American Governments, the capital for its completion would be readily furnished from this country and Europe, which might, failing such guaranties, prove inaccessible.

Diplomatic relations with Chile have also been strengthened by the reception of a minister from that country.

The war between Peru, Bolivia, and Chile still continues. The United States have not deemed it proper to interpose in the matter further than to convey to all the Governments concerned the assurance that the friendly offices of the Government of the United States for the restoration of peace upon an honorable basis will be extended in case the belligerents shall exhibit a readiness to accept them.

Cordial relations continue with Brazil and the Argentine Republic, and trade with those countries is improving. A provision for regular and more frequent mail communication, in our own ships, between the ports of this country and the nations of South America seems to me to deserve the attention of Congress as an essential precursor of an enlargement of our commerce with them and an extension of our carrying trade.

A recent revolution in Venezuela has been followed by the establishment of a provisional government. This government has not yet been formally recognized, and it is deemed desirable to await the proposed action of the people which is expected to give it the sanction of constitutional forms.

A naval vessel has been sent to the Samoan Islands to make surveys and take possession of the privileges ceded to the United States by Samoa in the harbor of Pago-Pago. A coaling station is to be established there, which will be convenient and useful to United States vessels.

The subject of opening diplomatic relations with Roumania and Servia, now become independent sovereignties, is at present under consideration, and is the subject of diplomatic correspondence.

There is a gratifying increase of trade with nearly all European and American countries, and it is believed that with judicious action in regard to its development it can and will be still more enhanced and that American products and manufactures will find new and expanding markets. The reports of diplomatic and consular officers upon this subject, under the system now adopted, have resulted in obtaining much valuable information, which has been and will continue to be laid before Congress and the public from time to time.

The third article of the treaty with Russia of March 30, 1867, by which Alaska was ceded to the United States, provides that the inhabitants of the ceded territory, with the exception of the uncivilized native tribes, shall be admitted to the enjoyment of all the rights of citizens of the United States and shall be maintained and protected in the free enjoyment of their liberty, property, and religion. The uncivilized tribes are subject to such laws and regulations as the United States may from time to time adopt in regard to the aboriginal tribes of that country.

Both the obligations of this treaty and the necessities of the people require that some organized form of government over the Territory of Alaska be adopted.

There appears to be no law for the arrest of persons charged with common-law offenses, such as assault, robbery, and murder, and no magistrate authorized to issue or execute process in such cases. Serious difficulties have already arisen from offenses of this character, not only among the original inhabitants, but among citizens of the United States and other countries who have engaged in mining, fishing, and other business operations within the territory. A bill authorizing the appointment of justices of the peace and constables and the arrest and detention of persons charged with criminal offenses, and providing for an appeal to United States courts for the district of Oregon in suitable cases, will at a proper time be submitted to Congress.

The attention of Congress is called to the annual report of the Secretary of the Treasury on the condition of the public finances.

The ordinary revenues from all sources for the fiscal year ended June 30, 1879, were $273,827,184.46; the ordinary expenditures for the same period were $266,947,883.53, leaving a surplus revenue for the year of $6,879,300.93.

The receipts for the present fiscal year, ending June 30, 1880, actual and estimated, are as follows: Actual receipts for the first quarter, commencing July 1, 1879, $79,843,663.61; estimated receipts for the remaining three quarters of the year, $208,156,336.39; total receipts for the current fiscal year, actual and estimated, $288,000,000.

The expenditures for the same period will be, actual and estimated, as follows: For the quarter commencing July 1, 1879, actual expenditures, $91,683,385.10; and for the remaining three quarters of the year the expenditures are estimated at $172,316,614.90, making the total expenditures $264,000,000, and leaving an estimated surplus revenue for the year ending June 30, 1880, of $24,000,000. The total receipts during the next fiscal year, ending June 30, 1881, estimated according to existing laws, will be $288,000,000, and the estimated ordinary expenditures for the same period will be $278,097,364.39, leaving a surplus of $9,902,635.61 for that year.

The large amount expended for arrears of pensions during the last and the present fiscal year, amounting to $21,747,249.60, has prevented the application of the full amount required by law to the sinking fund for the current year; but these arrears having been substantially paid, it is believed that the sinking fund can hereafter be maintained without any change of existing law.

The Secretary of War reports that the War Department estimates for the fiscal year ending June 30, 1881, are $40,380,428.93, the same being for a less sum of money than any annual estimate rendered to Congress from that Department during a period of at least twelve years.

He concurs with the General of the Army in recommending such legislation as will authorize the enlistment of the full number of 25,000 men for the line of the Army, exclusive of the 3,463 men required for detached duty, and therefore not available for service in the field.

He also recommends that Congress be asked to provide by law for the disposition of a large number of abandoned military posts and reservations, which, though very valuable in themselves, have been rendered useless for military purposes by the advance of civilization and settlement.

He unites with the Quartermaster-General in recommending that an appropriation be made for the construction of a cheap and perfectly fireproof building for the safe storage of a vast amount of money accounts, vouchers, claims, and other valuable records now in the Quartermaster-General's Office, and exposed to great risk of total destruction by fire.

He also recommends, in conformity with the views of the Judge-Advocate-General, some declaratory legislation in reference to the military statute of limitations as applied to the crime of desertion. In these several recommendations I concur.

The Secretary of War further reports that the work for the improvement of the South Pass of the Mississippi River, under contract with Mr. James B. Eads, made in pursuance of an act of Congress, has been prosecuted during the past year with a greater measure of success in the attainment of results than during any previous year. The channel through the South Pass, which at the beginning of operations in June, 1875, had a depth of only 7 1/2 feet of water, had on the 8th of July, 1879, a minimum depth of 26 feet, having a width of not less than 200 feet and a central depth of 30 feet. Payments have been made in accordance with the statute, as the work progressed, amounting in the aggregate to $4,250,000; and further payments will become due, as provided by the statute, in the event of success in maintaining the channel now secured.

The reports of the General of the Army and of his subordinates present a full and detailed account of the military operations for the suppression of hostilities among the Indians of the Ute and Apache tribes, and praise is justly awarded to the officers and troops engaged for promptness, skill, and courage displayed.

The past year has been one of almost unbroken peace and quiet on the Mexican frontier, and there is reason to believe that the efforts of this Government and of Mexico to maintain order in that region will prove permanently successful.

This Department was enabled during the past year to find temporary, though crowded, accommodations and a safe depository for a portion of its records in the completed east wing of the building designed for the State, War, and Navy Departments. The construction of the north wing of the building, a part of the structure intended for the use of the War Department, is being carried forward with all possible dispatch, and the work should receive from Congress such liberal appropriations as will secure its speedy completion.

The report of the Secretary of the Navy shows continued improvement in that branch of the service during the last fiscal year. Extensive repairs have been made upon vessels, and two new ships have been completed and made ready for sea.

The total expenditures of the year ended June 30, 1879, including specific appropriations not estimated for by the Department, were $13,555,710.09. The expenses chargeable to the year, after deducting the amount of these specific appropriations, were $13,343,317.79; but this is subject to a reduction of $283,725.99, that amount having been drawn upon warrants, but not paid out during the year. The amount of appropriations applicable to the last fiscal year was $14,538,646.17. There was, therefore, a balance of $1,479,054.37 remaining unexpended and to the credit of the Department on June 30, 1879. The estimates for the fiscal year ending June 30, 1881, are $14,864,147.95, which exceeds the appropriations for the present fiscal year $361,897.28. The reason for this increase is explained in the Secretary's report. The appropriations available for the present fiscal year are $14,502,250.67, which will, in the opinion of the Secretary, answer all the ordinary demands of the service. The amount drawn from the Treasury from July 1 to November 1, 1879 was $5,770,404.12, of which $1,095,440.33 has been refunded, leaving as the expenditure for that period $4,674,963.79. If the expenditures of the remaining two-thirds of the year do not exceed the proportion for these four months, there will remain unexpended at the end of the year $477,359.30 of the current appropriations. The report of the Secretary shows the gratifying fact that among all the disbursing officers of the Pay Corps of the Navy there is not one who is a defaulter to the extent of a single dollar. I unite with him in recommending the removal of the observatory to a more healthful location. That institution reflects credit upon the nation, and has obtained the approbation of scientific men in all parts of the world. Its removal from its present location would not only be conducive to the health of its officers and professors, but would greatly increase its usefulness.

The appropriation for judicial expenses, which has heretofore been made for the Department of Justice in gross, was subdivided at the last session of Congress, and no appropriation whatever was made for the payment of the fees of marshals and their deputies, either in the service of process or for the discharge of other duties; and since June 30 these officers have continued the performance of their duties without compensation from the Government, taking upon themselves the necessary incidental outlays, as well as rendering their own services. In only a few unavoidable instances has the proper execution of the process of the United States failed by reason of the absence of the requisite appropriation. This course of official conduct on the part of these officers, highly creditable to their fidelity, was advised by the Attorney-General, who informed them, however, that they would necessarily have to rely for their compensation upon the prospect of future legislation by Congress. I therefore especially recommend that immediate appropriation be made by Congress for this purpose.

The act making the principal appropriation for the Department of Justice at previous sessions has uniformly contained the following clause: And for defraying the expenses which my be incurred in the enforcement of the act approved February 28, 1871, entitled "An act to amend an act approved May 31, 1870, entitled 'An act to enforce the rights of citizens of the United States to vote in the several States of this Union, and for other purposes,'" or any acts amendatory thereof or supplementary thereto. No appropriation was made for this purpose for the current year. As no general election for Members of Congress occurred, the omission was a matter of little practical importance. Such election will, however, take place during the ensuing year, and the appropriation made for the pay of marshals and deputies should be sufficient to embrace compensation for the services they may be required to perform at such elections.

The business of the Supreme Court is at present largely in arrears. It can not be expected that more causes can be decided than are now disposed of in its annual session, or that by any assiduity the distinguished magistrates who compose the court can accomplish more than is now done. In the courts of many of the circuits also the business has increased to such an extent that the delay of justice will call the attention of Congress to an appropriate remedy. It is believed that all is done in each circuit which can fairly be expected from its judicial force. The evils arising from delay are less heavily felt by the United States than by private suitors, as its causes are advanced by the courts when it is seen that they involve the discussion of questions of a public character.

The remedy suggested by the Attorney-General is the appointment of additional circuit judges and the creation of an intermediate court of errors and appeals, which shall relieve the Supreme Court of a part of its jurisdiction, while a larger force is also obtained for the performance of circuit duties.

I commend this suggestion to the consideration of Congress. It would seem to afford a complete remedy, and would involve, if ten additional circuit judges are appointed, an expenditure, at the present rate of salaries, of not more than $60,000 a year, which would certainly be small in comparison with the objects to be attained.

The report of the Postmaster-General bears testimony to the general revival of business throughout the country. The receipts of the Post-Office Department for the fiscal year ended June 30, 1879, were $30,041,982.86, being $764,465.91 more than the revenues of the preceding year. The amount realized from the sale of postage stamps, stamped envelopes, and postal cards was $764,465.91 more than in the preceding year, and

$2,387,559.23 more than in 1877. The expenditures of the Department were $33,449,899.45, of which the sum of $376,461.63 was paid on liabilities incurred in preceding years.

The expenditures during the year were $801,209.77 less than in the preceding year. This reduction is to be attributed mainly to the operation of the law passed June 17, 1878, changing the compensation of postmasters from a commission on the value of stamps sold to a commission on stamps canceled.

The amount drawn from the Treasury on appropriations, in addition to the revenues of the Department, was $3,031,454.96, being $2,276,197.86 less than in the preceding year.

The expenditures for the fiscal year ending June 30, 1881, are estimated at $39,920,900 and the receipts from all sources at $32,210,000, leaving a deficiency to be appropriated for out of the Treasury of $7,710,900.

The relations of the Department with railroad companies have been harmonized, notwithstanding the general reduction by Congress of their compensation by the appropriation for special facilities, and the railway post-office lines have been greatly extended, especially in the Southern States. The interests of the Railway Mail Service and of the public would be greatly promoted and the expenditures could be more readily controlled by the classification of the employees of the Railway Mail Service as recommended by the Postmaster-General, the appropriation for salaries, with respect to which the maximum limit is already fixed by law, to be made in gross.

The Postmaster-General recommends an amendment of the law regulating the increase of compensation for increased service and increased speed on star routes, so as to enable him to advertise for proposals for such increased service and speed. He also suggests the advantages to accrue to the commerce of the country from the enactment of a general law authorizing contracts with American-built steamers, carrying the American flag, for transporting the mail between ports of the United States and ports of the West Indies and South America, at a fixed maximum price per mile, the amount to be expended being regulated by annual appropriations, in like manner with the amount paid for the domestic star service.

The arrangement made by the Postmaster-General and the Secretary of the Treasury for the collection of duty upon books received in the mail from foreign countries has proved so satisfactory in its practical operation that the recommendation is now made that Congress shall extend the provisions of the act of March 3, 1879, under which this arrangement was made, so as to apply to all other dutiable articles received in the mails from foreign countries.

The reports of the Secretary of the Interior and of the Commissioner of Indian Affairs, setting forth the present state of our relations with the

Indian tribes on our territory, the measures taken to advance their civilization and prosperity, and the progress already achieved by them, will be found of more than ordinary interest. The general conduct of our Indian population has been so satisfactory that the occurrence of two disturbances, which resulted in bloodshed and destruction of property, is all the more to be lamented.

The history of the outbreak on the White River Ute Reservation, in western Colorado, has become so familiar by elaborate reports in the public press that its remarkable incidents need not be stated here in detail. It is expected that the settlement of this difficulty will lead to such arrangements as will prevent further hostile contact between the Indians and the border settlements in western Colorado.

The other disturbance occurred at the Mescalero Agency, in New Mexico, where Victoria, at the head of a small band of marauders, after committing many atrocities, being vigorously chased by a military force, made his way across the Mexican border and is now on foreign soil.

While these occurrences, in which a comparatively small number of Indians were engaged, are most deplorable, a vast majority of our Indian population have fully justified the expectations of those who believe that by humane and peaceful influences the Indian can be led to abandon the habits of savage life and to develop a capacity for useful and civilized occupations. What they have already accomplished in the pursuit of agricultural and mechanical work, the remarkable success which has attended the experiment of employing as freighters a class of Indians hitherto counted among the wildest and most intractable, and the general and urgent desire expressed by them for the education of their children may be taken as sufficient proof that they will be found capable of accomplishing much more if they continue to be wisely and fairly guided. The "Indian policy" sketched in the report of the Secretary of the Interior, the object of which is to make liberal provision for the education of Indian youth, to settle the Indians upon farm lots in severalty, to give them title in fee to their farms, inalienable for a certain number of years, and when their wants are thus provided for to dispose by sale of the lands on their reservations not occupied and used by them, a fund to be formed out of the proceeds for the benefit of the Indians, which will gradually relieve the Government of the expenses now provided for by annual appropriations, must commend itself as just and beneficial to the Indians, and as also calculated to remove those obstructions which the existence of large reservations presents to the settlement and development of the country. I therefore earnestly recommend the enactment of a law enabling the Government to give Indians a title in fee, inalienable for twenty-five years, to the farm lands assigned to them by allotment. I also repeat the recommendation made in my first annual message, that a law be passed admitting Indians who can give satisfactory proof of having by their own labor supported their families for a number of years, and who are willing to detach themselves from their tribal relations, to the benefit of the homestead act, and to grant them patents containing the same provision of inalienability for a certain period.

The experiment of sending a number of Indian children of both sexes to the Hampton Normal and Agricultural Institute, in Virginia, to receive an elementary English education and practical instruction in farming and other useful industries, has led to results so promising that it was thought expedient to turn over the cavalry barracks at Carlisle, in Pennsylvania, to the Interior Department for the establishment of an Indian school on a larger scale. This school has now 158 pupils, selected from various tribes, and is in full operation. Arrangements are also made for the education of a number of Indian boys and girls belonging to tribes on the Pacific Slope in a similar manner, at Forest Grove, in Oregon. These institutions will commend themselves to the liberality of Congress and to the philanthropic munificence of the American people.

Last spring information was received of the organization of an extensive movement in the Western States, the object of which was the occupation by unauthorized persons of certain lands in the Indian Territory ceded by the Cherokees to the Government for the purpose of settlement by other Indian tribes.

On the 26th of April I issued a proclamation warning all persons against participation in such an attempt, and by the cooperation of a military force the invasion was promptly checked. It is my purpose to protect the rights of the Indian inhabitants of that Territory to the full extent of the executive power; but it would be unwise to ignore the fact that a territory so large and so fertile, with a population so sparse and with so great a wealth of unused resources, will be found more exposed to the repetition of such attempts as happened this year when the surrounding States are more densely settled and the westward movement of our population looks still more eagerly for fresh lands to occupy. Under such circumstances the difficulty of maintaining the Indian Territory in its present state will greatly increase, and the Indian tribes inhabiting it would do well to prepare for such a contingency. I therefore fully approve of the advice given to them by the Secretary of the Interior on a recent occasion, to divide among themselves in severalty as large a quantity of their lands as they can cultivate; to acquire individual title in fee instead of their present tribal ownership in common, and to consider in what manner the balance of their lands may be disposed of by the Government for their benefit. By adopting such a policy they would more certainly secure for themselves the value of their possessions, and at the same time promote their progress in civilization and prosperity, than by endeavoring to perpetuate the present state of things in the Territory.

The question whether a change in the control of the Indian service should be made was in the Forty-fifth Congress referred to a joint committee of both Houses for inquiry and report. In my last annual message I expressed the hope that the decision of that question, then in prospect, would "arrest further agitation of this subject, such agitation being apt to produce a disturbing effect upon the service as well as on the Indians themselves." Since then, the committee having reported, the question has been decided in the negative by a vote in the House of Representatives.

For the reasons here stated, and in view of the fact that further uncertainty on this point will be calculated to obstruct other much-needed legislation, to weaken the discipline of the service, and to unsettle salutary measures now in progress for the government and improvement of the Indians, I respectfully recommend that the decision arrived at by Congress at its last session be permitted to stand.

The efforts made by the Department of the Interior to arrest the depredations on the timber lands of the United States have been continued, and have met with considerable success. A large number of cases of trespass have been prosecuted in the courts of the United States; others have been settled, the trespassers offering to make payment to the Government for the value of the timber taken by them. The proceeds of these prosecutions and settlements turned into the Treasury far exceed in amount the sums appropriated by Congress for this purpose. A more important result, however, consists in the fact that the destruction of our public forests by depredation, although such cases still occur, has been greatly reduced in extent, and it is probable that if the present policy is vigorously pursued and sufficient provision to that end is made by Congress such trespasses, at least those on a large scale, can be entirely suppressed, except in the Territories, where timber for the daily requirements of the population can not, under the present state of the law, be otherwise obtained. I therefore earnestly invite the attention of Congress to the recommendation made by the Secretary of the Interior, that a law be enacted enabling the Government to sell timber from the public lands without conveying the fee, where such lands are principally valuable for the timber thereon, such sales to be so regulated as to conform to domestic wants and business requirements, while at the same time guarding against a sweeping destruction of the forests. The enactment of such a law appears to become a more pressing necessity every day.

My recommendations in former messages are renewed in favor of enlarging the facilities of the Department of Agriculture. Agriculture is the leading interest and the permanent industry of our people. It is to the abundance of agricultural production, as compared with our home consumption, and the largely increased and highly profitable market abroad which we have enjoyed in recent years, that we are mainly indebted for our present prosperity as a people. We must look for its continued maintenance to the same substantial resource. There is no branch of industry in which labor, directed by scientific knowledge, yields such increased production in comparison with unskilled labor, and no branch of the public service to which the encouragement of liberal appropriations can be more appropriately extended. The omission to render such aid is not a wise economy, but, on the contrary, undoubtedly results in losses of immense sums annually that might be saved through well-directed efforts by the Government to promote this vital interest.

The results already accomplished with the very limited means heretofore placed at the command of the Department of Agriculture is an earnest of what may be expected with increased appropriations for the several purposes indicated in the report of the Commissioner, with a view to placing the Department upon a footing which will enable it to prosecute more effectively the objects for which it is established.

Appropriations are needed for a more complete laboratory, for the establishment of a veterinary division and a division of forestry, and for an increase of force.

The requirements for these and other purposes, indicated in the report of the Commissioner under the head of the immediate necessities of the Department, will not involve any expenditure of money that the country can not with propriety now undertake in the interests of agriculture.

It is gratifying to learn from the Bureau of Education the extent to which educational privileges throughout the United States have been advanced during the year. No more fundamental responsibility rests upon Congress than that of devising appropriate measures of financial aid to education, supplemental to local action in the States and Territories and in the District of Columbia. The wise forethought of the founders of our Government has not only furnished the basis for the support of the common-school systems of the newer States, but laid the foundations for the maintenance of their universities and colleges of agriculture and the mechanic arts. Measures in accordance with this traditional policy, for the further benefit of all these interests and the extension of the same advantages to every portion of the country, it is hoped will receive your favorable consideration.

To preserve and perpetuate the national literature should be among the foremost cares of the National Legislature. The library gathered at the Capitol still remains unprovided with any suitable accommodations for its rapidly increasing stores. The magnitude and importance of the collection, increased as it is by the deposits made under the law of copyright, by domestic and foreign exchanges, and by the scientific library of the Smithsonian Institution, call for building accommodations which shall be at once adequate and fireproof. The location of such a public building, which should provide for the pressing necessities of the present and for the vast increase of the nation's books in the future, is a matter which addresses itself to the discretion of Congress. It is earnestly recommended as a measure which should unite all suffrages and which should no longer be delayed.

The joint commission created by the act of Congress of August 2, 1876, for the purpose of supervising and directing the completion of the Washington National Monument, of which commission the President is a member, has given careful attention to this subject, and already the strengthening of the foundation has so far progressed as to insure the entire success of this part of the work. A massive layer of masonry has been introduced below the original foundation, widening the base, increasing the stability of the structure, and rendering it possible to carry the shaft to completion. It is earnestly recommended that such further appropriations be made for the continued prosecution of the work as may be necessary for the completion of this national monument at an early day.

In former messages, impressed with the importance of the subject, I have taken occasion to commend to Congress the adoption of a generous policy toward the District of Columbia. The report of the Commissioners of the District, herewith transmitted, contains suggestions and recommendations, to all of which I earnestly invite your careful attention. I ask your early and favorable consideration of the views which they express as to the urgent need of legislation for the reclamation of the marshes of the Potomac and its Eastern Branch within the limits of the city, and for the repair of the streets of the capital, heretofore laid with wooden blocks and now by decay rendered almost impassable and a source of imminent danger to the health of its citizens. The means at the disposal of the Commissioners are wholly inadequate for the accomplishment of these important works, and should be supplemented by timely appropriations from the Federal Treasury.

The filling of the flats in front of the city will add to the adjacent lands and parks now owned by the United States a large and valuable domain, sufficient, it is thought, to reimburse its entire cost, and will also, as an incidental result, secure the permanent improvement of the river for the purposes of navigation.

The Constitution having invested Congress with supreme and exclusive jurisdiction over the District of Columbia, its citizens must of necessity look to Congress alone for all needful legislation affecting their interests; and as the territory of this District is the common property of the people of the United States, who equally with its resident citizens are interested in the prosperity of their capital, I can not doubt that you will be amply sustained by the general voice of the country in any measures you may adopt for this purpose.

I also invite the favorable consideration of Congress to the wants of the public schools of this District, as exhibited in the report of the

Commissioners. While the number of pupils is rapidly increasing, no adequate provision exists for a corresponding increase of school accommodation, and the Commissioners are without the means to meet this urgent need. A number of the buildings now used for school purposes are rented, and are in important particulars unsuited for the purpose. The cause of popular education in the District of Columbia is surely entitled to the same consideration at the hands of the National Government as in the several States and Territories, to which munificent grants of the public lands have been made for the endowment of schools and universities.

THE FOURTH ADDRESS

State of the Union Address
Rutherford B. Hayes
December 6, 1880

Fellow-Citizens of the Senate and House of Representatives:

I congratulate you on the continued and increasing prosperity of our country. By the favor of Divine Providence we have been blessed during the past year with health, with abundant harvests, with profitable employment for all our people, and with contentment at home, and with peace and friendship with other nations. The occurrence of the twenty-fourth election of Chief Magistrate has afforded another opportunity to the people of the United States to exhibit to the world a significant example of the peaceful and safe transmission of the power and authority of government from the public servants whose terms of office are about to expire to their newly chosen successors. This example can not fail to impress profoundly thoughtful people of other countries with the advantages which republican institutions afford. The immediate, general, and cheerful acquiescence of all good citizens in the result of the election gives gratifying assurance to our country and to its friends throughout the world that a government based on the free consent of an intelligent and patriotic people possesses elements of strength, stability, and permanency not found in any other form of government.

Continued opposition to the full and free enjoyment of the rights of citizenship conferred upon the colored people by the recent amendments to the Constitution still prevails in several of the late slaveholding States. It has, perhaps, not been manifested in the recent election to any large extent in acts of violence or intimidation. It has, however, by fraudulent practices in connection with the ballots, with the regulations as to the places and manner of voting, and with counting, returning, and canvassing the votes cast, been successful in defeating the exercise of the right preservative of all rights—the right of suffrage—which the Constitution expressly confers upon our enfranchised citizens.

It is the desire of the good people of the whole country that sectionalism as a factor in our politics should disappear. They prefer that no section of the country should be united in solid opposition to any other section. The disposition to refuse a prompt and hearty obedience to the equal-rights amendments to the Constitution is all that now stands in the way of a complete obliteration of sectional lines in our political contests. As long as either of these amendments is flagrantly violated or disregarded, it is safe to assume that the people who placed them in the Constitution, as embodying the legitimate results of the war for the Union, and who believe them to be wise and necessary, will continue to act together and to insist that they shall be obeyed. The paramount question still is as to the enjoyment of the fight by every American citizen who has the requisite qualifications to freely cast his vote and to have it honestly counted. With this question rightly settled, the country will be relieved of the contentions of the past; bygones will indeed be bygones, and political and party issues, with respect to economy and efficiency of administration, internal improvements, the tariff, domestic taxation, education, finance, and other important subjects, will then receive their full share of attention; but resistance to and nullification of the results of the war will unite together in resolute purpose for their support all who maintain the authority of the Government and the perpetuity of the Union, and who adequately appreciate the value of the victory achieved. This determination proceeds from no hostile sentiment or feeling to any part of the people of our country or to any of their interests. The inviolability of the amendments rests upon the fundamental principle of our Government. They are the solemn expression of the will of the people of the United States.

The sentiment that the constitutional rights of all our citizens must be maintained does not grow weaker. It will continue to control the Government of the country. Happily, the history of the late election shows that in many parts of the country where opposition to the fifteenth amendment has heretofore prevailed it is diminishing, and is likely to cease altogether if firm and well-considered action is taken by Congress. I trust the House of Representatives and the Senate, which have the right to judge of the elections, returns, and qualifications of their own members, will see to it that every case of violation of the letter or spirit of the fifteenth amendment is thoroughly investigated, and that no benefit from such violation shall accrue to any person or party. It will be the duty of the

Executive, with sufficient appropriations for the purpose, to prosecute unsparingly all who have been engaged in depriving citizens of the rights guaranteed to them by the Constitution.

It is not, however, to be forgotten that the best and surest guaranty of the primary rights of citizenship is to be found in that capacity for self-protection which can belong only to a people whose right to universal suffrage is supported by universal education. The means at the command of the local and State authorities are in many cases wholly inadequate to furnish free instruction to all who need it. This is especially true where before emancipation the education of the people was neglected or prevented, in the interest of slavery. Firmly convinced that the subject of popular education deserves the earnest attention of the people of the whole country, with a view to wise and comprehensive action by the Government of the United States, I respectfully recommend that Congress, by suitable legislation and with proper safeguards, supplement the local educational funds in the several States where the grave duties and responsibilities of citizenship have been devolved on uneducated people by devoting to the purpose grants of the public lands and, if necessary, by appropriations from the Treasury of the United States. Whatever Government can fairly do to promote free popular education ought to be done. Wherever general education is found, peace, virtue, and social order prevail and civil and religious liberty are secure.

In my former annual messages I have asked the attention of Congress to the urgent necessity of a reformation of the civil-service system of the Government. My views concerning the dangers of patronage, or appointments for personal or partisan considerations, have been strengthened by my observation and experience in the Executive office, and I believe these dangers threaten the stability of the Government. Abuses so serious in their nature can not be permanently tolerated. They tend to become more alarming with the enlargement of administrative service, as the growth of the country in population increases the number of officers and placemen employed.

The reasons are imperative for the adoption of fixed rules for the regulation of appointments, promotions, and removals, establishing a uniform method having exclusively in view in every instance the attainment of the best qualifications for the position in question. Such a method alone is consistent with the equal rights of all citizens and the most economical and efficient administration of the public business.

Competitive examinations in aid of impartial appointments and promotions have been conducted for some years past in several of the Executive Departments, and by my direction this system has been adopted in the custom-houses and post-offices of the larger cities of the country. In the city of New York over 2,000 positions in the civil service have been subject in their appointments and tenure of place to the operation of published rules for this purpose during the past two years. The results of these practical trials have been very satisfactory, and have confirmed my opinion in favor of this system of selection. All are subjected to the same tests, and the result is free from prejudice by personal favor or partisan influence. It secures for the position applied for the best qualifications attainable among the competing applicants. It is an effectual protection from the pressure of importunity, which under any other course pursued largely exacts the time and attention of appointing officers, to their great detriment in the discharge of other official duties preventing the abuse of the service for the mere furtherance of private or party purposes, and leaving the employee of the Government, freed from the obligations imposed by patronage, to depend solely upon merit for retention and advancement, and with this constant incentive to exertion and improvement.

These invaluable results have been attained in a high degree in the offices where the rules for appointment by competitive examination have been applied.

A method which has so approved itself by experimental tests at points where such tests may be fairly considered conclusive should be extended to all subordinate positions under the Government. I believe that a strong and growing public sentiment demands immediate measures for securing and enforcing the highest possible efficiency in the civil service and its protection from recognized abuses, and that the experience referred to has demonstrated the feasibility of such measures.

The examinations in the custom-houses and post-offices have been held under many embarrassments and without provision for compensation for the extra labor performed by the officers who have conducted them, and whose commendable interest in the improvement of the public service has induced this devotion of time and labor without pecuniary reward. A continuance of these labors gratuitously ought not to be expected, and without an appropriation by Congress for compensation it is not practicable to extend the system of examinations generally throughout the civil service. It is also highly important that all such examinations should be conducted upon a uniform system and under general supervision. Section 1753 of the Revised Statutes authorizes the President to prescribe the regulations for admission to the civil service of the United States, and for this purpose to employ suitable persons to conduct the requisite inquiries with reference to "the fitness of each candidate, in respect to age, health, character, knowledge, and ability for the branch of service into which he seeks to enter;" but the law is practically inoperative for want of the requisite appropriation.

I therefore recommend an appropriation of $25,000 per annum to meet the expenses of a commission, to be appointed by the President in accordance with the terms of this section, whose duty it shall be to devise a just, uniform, and efficient system of competitive examinations and to supervise the application of the same throughout the entire civil service of the Government. I am persuaded that the facilities which such a commission will afford for testing the fitness of those who apply for office will not only be as welcome a relief to members of Congress as it will be to the President and heads of Departments, but that it will also greatly tend to remove the causes of embarrassment which now inevitably and constantly attend the conflicting claims of patronage between the legislative and executive departments. The most effectual check upon the pernicious competition of influence and official favoritism in the bestowal of office will be the substitution of an open competition of merit between the applicants, in which everyone can make his own record with the assurance that his success will depend upon this alone.

I also recommend such legislation as, while leaving every officer as free as any other citizen to express his political opinions and to use his means for their advancement, shall also enable him to feel as safe as any private citizen in refusing all demands upon his salary for political purposes. A law which should thus guarantee true liberty and justice to all who are engaged in the public service, and likewise contain stringent provisions against the use of official authority to coerce the political action of private citizens or of official subordinates, is greatly to be desired.

The most serious obstacle, however, to an improvement of the civil service, and especially to a reform in the method of appointment and removal, has been found to be the practice, under what is known as the spoils system, by which the appointing power has been so largely encroached upon by members of Congress. The first step in the reform of the civil service must be a complete divorce between Congress and the Executive in the matter of appointments. The corrupting doctrine that "to the victors belong the spoils" is inseparable from Congressional patronage as the established rule and practice of parties in power. It comes to be understood by applicants for office and by the people generally that Representatives and Senators are entitled to disburse the patronage of their respective districts and States. It is not necessary to recite at length the evils resulting from this invasion of the Executive functions. The true principles of Government on the subject of appointments to office, as stated in the national conventions of the leading parties of the country, have again and again been approved by the American people, and have not been called in question in any quarter. These authentic expressions of public opinion upon this all-important subject are the statement of principles that belong to the constitutional structure of the Government. Under the Constitution the President and heads of Departments are to make nominations for office. The Senate is to advise and consent to appointments, and the House of Representatives is to accuse and prosecute faithless officers. The best interest of the public service demands that these distinctions be respected; that Senators and Representatives, who may be judges and accusers, should not dictate appointments to office. To this end the cooperation of the legislative department of the Government is required alike by the necessities of the case and by public opinion. Members of Congress will not be relieved from the demands made upon them with reference to appointments to office until by legislative enactment the pernicious practice is condemned and forbidden.

It is therefore recommended that an act be passed defining the relations of members of Congress with respect to appointment to office by the President; and I also recommend that the provisions of section 1767 and of the sections following of the Revised Statutes, comprising the tenure-of-office act of March 2, 1867, be repealed.

Believing that to reform the system and methods of the civil service in our country is one of the highest and most imperative duties of statesmanship, and that it can be permanently done only by the cooperation of the legislative and executive departments of the Government, I again commend the whole subject to your considerate attention.

It is the recognized duty and purpose of the people of the United States to suppress polygamy where it now exists in our Territories and to prevent its extension. Faithful and zealous efforts have been made by the United States authorities in Utah to enforce the laws against it. Experience has shown that the legislation upon this subject, to be effective, requires extensive modification and amendment. The longer action is delayed the more difficult it will be to accomplish what is desired. Prompt and decided measures are necessary. The Mormon sectarian organization which upholds polygamy has the whole power of making and executing the local legislation of the Territory. By its control of the grand and petit juries it possesses large influence over the administration of justice. Exercising, as the heads of this sect do, the local political power of the Territory, they are able to make effective their hostility to the law of Congress on the subject of polygamy, and, in fact, do prevent its enforcement. Polygamy will not be abolished if the enforcement of the law depends on those who practice and uphold the crime. It can only be suppressed by taking away the political power of the sect which encourages and sustains it.

The power of Congress to enact suitable laws to protect the Territories is ample. It is not a case for halfway measures. The political power of the Mormon sect is increasing. It controls now one of our wealthiest and most populous Territories. It is extending steadily into other Territories. Wherever it goes it establishes polygamy and sectarian political power. The sanctity of marriage and the family relation are the corner stone of our American society and civilization. Religious liberty and the separation of church and state are among the elementary ideas of free institutions. To reestablish the interests and principles which polygamy and Mormonism have imperiled, and to fully reopen to intelligent and virtuous immigrants of all creeds that part of our domain which has been in a great degree closed to general immigration by intolerant and immoral institutions, it is recommended that the government of the Territory of Utah be reorganized. I recommend that Congress provide for the government of Utah by a governor and judges, or commissioners, appointed by the President and confirmed by the Senate—a government analogous to the provisional government established for the territory northwest of the Ohio by the ordinance of 1787. If, however, it is deemed best to continue the existing form of local government, I recommend that the right to vote, hold office, and sit on juries in the Territory of Utah be confined to those who neither practice nor uphold polygamy. If thorough measures are adopted, it is believed that within a few years the evils which now afflict Utah will be eradicated, and that this Territory will in good time become one of the most prosperous and attractive of the new States of the Union.

Our relations with all foreign countries have been those of undisturbed peace, and have presented no occasion for concern as to their continued maintenance.

My anticipation of an early reply from the British Government to the demand of indemnity to our fishermen for the injuries suffered by that industry at Fortune Bay in January, 1878, which I expressed in my last annual message, was disappointed. This answer was received only in the latter part of April in the present year, and when received exhibited a failure of accord between the two Governments as to the measure of the inshore fishing privilege secured to our fishermen by the treaty of Washington of so serious a character that I made it the subject of a communication to Congress, in which I recommended the adoption of the measures which seemed to me proper to be taken by this Government in maintenance of the rights accorded to our fishermen under the treaty and toward securing an indemnity for the injury these interests had suffered. A bill to carry out these recommendations was under consideration by the House of Representatives at the time of the adjournment of Congress in June last.

Within a few weeks I have received a communication from Her Majesty's Government renewing the consideration of the subject, both of the indemnity for the injuries at Fortune Bay and of the interpretation of the treaty in which the previous correspondence had shown the two Governments to be at variance. Upon both these topics the disposition toward a friendly agreement is manifested by a recognition of our right to an indemnity for the transaction at Fortune Bay, leaving the measure of such indemnity to further conference, and by an assent to the view of this Government, presented in the previous correspondence, that the regulation of conflicting interests of the shore fishery of the provincial seacoasts and the vessel fishery of our fishermen should be made the subject of conference and concurrent arrangement between the two Governments.

I sincerely hope that the basis may be found for a speedy adjustment of the very serious divergence of views in the interpretation of the fishery clauses of the treaty of Washington, which, as the correspondence between the two Governments stood at the close of the last session of Congress, seemed to be irreconcilable.

In the important exhibition of arts and industries which was held last year at Sydney, New South Wales, as well as in that now in progress at Melbourne, the United States have been efficiently and honorably represented. The exhibitors from this country at the former place received a large number of awards in some of the most considerable departments, and the participation of the United States was recognized by a special mark of distinction. In the exhibition at Melbourne the share taken by our country is no less notable, and an equal degree of success is confidently expected.

The state of peace and tranquillity now enjoyed by all the nations of the continent of Europe has its favorable influence upon our diplomatic and commercial relations with them. We have concluded and ratified a convention with the French Republic for the settlement of claims of the citizens of either country against the other. Under this convention a commission, presided over by a distinguished publicist, appointed in pursuance of the request of both nations by His Majesty the Emperor of Brazil, has been organized and has begun its sessions in this city. A congress to consider means for the protection of industrial property has recently been in session in Paris, to which I have appointed the ministers of the United States in France and in Belgium as delegates. The International Commission upon Weights and Measures also continues its work in Paris. I invite your attention to the necessity of an appropriation to be made in time to enable this Government to comply with its obligations under the metrical convention.

Our friendly relations with the German Empire continue without interruption. At the recent International Exhibition of Fish and Fisheries at Berlin the participation of the United States, notwithstanding the haste with which the commission was forced to make its preparations, was extremely successful and meritorious, winning for private exhibitors numerous awards of a high class and for the country at large the principal prize of honor offered by His Majesty the Emperor. The results of this great success can not but be advantageous to this important and growing industry. There have been some questions raised between the two Governments as to the proper effect and interpretation of our treaties of naturalization, but recent dispatches from our minister at Berlin show that favorable progress is making toward an understanding in accordance with the views of this

Government, which makes and admits no distinction whatever between the rights of a native and a naturalized citizen of the United States. In practice the complaints of molestation suffered by naturalized citizens abroad have never been fewer than at present.

There is nothing of importance to note in our unbroken friendly relations with the Governments of Austria-Hungary, Russia, Portugal, Sweden and Norway, Switzerland, Turkey, and Greece.

During the last summer several vessels belonging to the merchant marine of this country, sailing in neutral waters of the West Indies, were fired at, boarded, and searched by an armed cruiser of the Spanish Government. The circumstances as reported involve not only a private injury to the persons concerned, but also seemed too little observant of the friendly relations existing for a century between this country and Spain. The wrong was brought to the attention of the Spanish Government in a serious protest and remonstrance, and the matter is undergoing investigation by the royal authorities with a view to such explanation or reparation as may be called for by the facts.

The commission sitting in this city for the adjudication of claims of our citizens against the Government of Spain is, I hope, approaching the termination of its labors.

The claims against the United States under the Florida treaty with Spain were submitted to Congress for its action at the late session, and I again invite your attention to this long-standing question, with a view to a final disposition of the matter.

At the invitation of the Spanish Government, a conference has recently been held at the city of Madrid to consider the subject of protection by foreign powers of native Moors in the Empire of Morocco. The minister of the United States in Spain was directed to take part in the deliberations of this conference, the result of which is a convention signed on behalf of all the powers represented. The instrument will be laid before the Senate for its consideration. The Government of the United States has also lost no opportunity to urge upon that of the Emperor of Morocco the necessity, in accordance with the humane and enlightened spirit of the age, of putting an end to the persecutions, which have been so prevalent in that country, of persons of a faith other than the Moslem, and especially of the Hebrew residents of Morocco.

The consular treaty concluded with Belgium has not yet been officially promulgated, owing to the alteration of a word in the text by the Senate of the United States, which occasioned a delay, during which the time allowed for ratification expired. The Senate will be asked to extend the period for ratification.

The attempt to negotiate a treaty of extradition with Denmark failed on account of the objection of the Danish Government to the usual clause providing that each nation should pay the expense of the arrest of the persons whose extradition it asks.

The provision made by Congress at its last session for the expense of the commission which had been appointed to enter upon negotiations with the Imperial Government of China on subjects of great interest to the relations of the two countries enabled the commissioners to proceed at once upon their mission. The Imperial Government was prepared to give prompt and respectful attention to the matters brought under negotiation, and the conferences proceeded with such rapidity and success that on the 17th of November last two treaties were signed at Peking, one relating to the introduction of Chinese into this country and one relating to commerce. Mr. Trescot, one of the commissioners, is now on his way home bringing the treaties, and it is expected that they will be received in season to be laid before the Senate early in January.

Our minister in Japan has negotiated a convention for the reciprocal relief of shipwrecked seamen. I take occasion to urge once more upon Congress the propriety of making provision for the erection of suitable fireproof buildings at the Japanese capital for the use of the American legation and the court-house and jail connected with it. The Japanese Government, with great generosity and courtesy, has offered for this purpose an eligible piece of land.

In my last annual message I invited the attention of Congress to the subject of the indemnity funds received some years ago from China and Japan. I renew the recommendation then made that whatever portions of these funds are due to American citizens should be promptly paid and the residue returned to the nations, respectively, to which they justly and equitably belong.

The extradition treaty with the Kingdom of the Netherlands, Which has been for some time in course of negotiation, has during the past year been concluded and duly ratified.

Relations of friendship and amity have been established between the Government of the United States and that of Roumania. We have sent a diplomatic representative to Bucharest, and have received at this capital the special envoy who has been charged by His Royal Highness Prince Charles to announce the independent sovereignty of Roumania. We hope for a speedy development of commercial relations between the two countries.

In my last annual message I expressed the hope that the prevalence of quiet on the border between this country and Mexico would soon become so assured as to justify the modification of the orders then in force to our military commanders in regard to crossing the frontier, without encouraging such disturbances as would endanger the peace of the two countries. Events moved in accordance with these expectations, and the orders were accordingly withdrawn, to the entire satisfaction of our own citizens and the

Mexican Government. Subsequently the peace of the border was again disturbed by a savage foray under the command of the Chief Victoria, but by the combined and harmonious action of the military forces of both countries his band has been broken up and substantially destroyed.

There is reason to believe that the obstacles which have so long prevented rapid and convenient communication between the United States and Mexico by railways are on the point of disappearing, and that several important enterprises of this character will soon be set on foot, which can not fail to contribute largely to the prosperity of both countries.

New envoys from Guatemala, Colombia, Bolivia, Venezuela, and Nicaragua have recently arrived at this capital, whose distinction and enlightenment afford the best guaranty of the continuance of friendly relations between ourselves and these sister Republics.

The relations between this Government and that of the United States of Colombia have engaged public attention during the past year, mainly by reason of the project of an interoceanic canal across the Isthmus of Panama, to be built by private capital under a concession from the Colombian Government for that purpose. The treaty obligations subsisting between the United States and Colombia, by which we guarantee the neutrality of the transit and the sovereignty and property of Colombia in the Isthmus, make it necessary that the conditions under which so stupendous a change in the region embraced in this guaranty should be effected—transforming, as it would, this Isthmus from a barrier between the Atlantic and Pacific oceans into a gateway and thoroughfare between them for the navies and the merchant ships of the world—should receive the approval of this Government, as being compatible with the discharge of these obligations on our part and consistent with our interests as the principal commercial power of the Western Hemisphere. The views which I expressed in a special message to Congress in March last in relation to this project I deem it my duty again to press upon your attention. Subsequent consideration has but confirmed the opinion "that it is the right and duty of the United States to assert and maintain such supervision and authority over any interoceanic canal across the isthmus that connects North and South America as will protect our national interest."

The war between the Republic of Chile on the one hand and the allied Republics of Peru and Bolivia on the other still continues. This Government has not felt called upon to interfere in a contest that is within the belligerent rights of the parties as independent states. We have, however, always held ourselves in readiness to aid in accommodating their difference, and have at different times reminded both belligerents of our willingness to render such service.

Our good offices in this direction were recently accepted by all the belligerents, and it was hoped they would prove efficacious; but I regret to announce that the measures which the ministers of the United States at Santiago and Lima were authorized to take with the view to bring about a peace were not successful. In the course of the war some questions have arisen affecting neutral rights. In all of these the ministers of the United States have, under their instructions, acted with promptness and energy in protection of American interests.

The relations of the United States with the Empire of Brazil continue to be most cordial, and their commercial intercourse steadily increases, to their mutual advantage.

The internal disorders with which the Argentine Republic has for some time past been afflicted, and which have more or less influenced its external trade, are understood to have been brought to a close. This happy result may be expected to redound to the benefit of the foreign commerce of that Republic, as well as to the development of its vast interior resources.

In Samoa the Government of King Malietoa, under the support and recognition of the consular representatives of the United States, Great Britain, and Germany, seems to have given peace and tranquillity to the islands. While it does not appear desirable to adopt as a whole the scheme of tripartite local government which has been proposed, the common interests of the three great treaty powers require harmony in their relations to the native frame of government, and this may be best secured by a simple diplomatic agreement between them. It would be well if the consular jurisdiction of our representative at Apia were increased in extent and importance so as to guard American interests in the surrounding and outlying islands of Oceanica.

The obelisk generously presented by the Khedive of Egypt to the city of New York has safely arrived in this country, and will soon be erected in that metropolis. A commission for the liquidation of the Egyptian debt has lately concluded its work, and this Government, at the earnest solicitation of the Khedive, has acceded to the provisions adopted by it, which will be laid before Congress for its information. A commission for the revision of the judicial code of the reform tribunal of Egypt is now in session in Cairo. Mr. Farman, consul-general, and J. M. Batchelder, esq., have been appointed as commissioners to participate in this work. The organization of the reform tribunals will probably be continued for another period of five years.

In pursuance of the act passed at the last session of Congress, invitations have been extended to foreign maritime states to join in a sanitary conference in Washington, beginning the 1st of January. The acceptance of this invitation by many prominent powers gives promise of success in this important measure, designed to establish a system of international notification by which the spread of infectious or epidemic diseases may be more effectively checked or prevented. The attention of Congress is invited to the necessary appropriations for carrying into effect the provisions of the act referred to.

The efforts of the Department of State to enlarge the trade and commerce of the United States, through the active agency of consular officers and through the dissemination of information obtained from them, have been unrelaxed. The interest in these efforts, as developed in our commercial communities, and the value of the information secured by this means to the trade and manufactures of the country were recognized by Congress at its last session, and provision was made for the more frequent publication of consular and other reports by the Department of State. The first issue of this publication has now been prepared, and subsequent issues may regularly be expected. The importance and interest attached to the reports of consular officers are witnessed by the general demand for them by all classes of merchants and manufacturers engaged in our foreign trade. It is believed that the system of such publications is deserving of the approval of Congress, and that the necessary appropriations for its continuance and enlargement will commend itself to your consideration.

The prosperous energies of our domestic industries and their immense production of the subjects of foreign commerce invite, and even require, an active development of the wishes and interests of our people in that direction. Especially important is it that our commercial relations with the Atlantic and Pacific coasts of South America, with the West Indies and the Gulf of Mexico, should be direct, and not through the circuit of European systems, and should be carried on in our own bottoms. The full appreciation of the opportunities which our front on the Pacific Ocean gives to commerce with Japan, China, and the East Indies, with Australia and the island groups which lie along these routes of navigation, should inspire equal efforts to appropriate to our own shipping and to administer by our own capital a due proportion of this trade. Whatever modifications of our regulations of trade and navigation may be necessary or useful to meet and direct these impulses to the enlargement of our exchanges and of our carrying trade I am sure the wisdom of Congress will be ready to supply. One initial measure, however, seems to me so clearly useful and efficient that I venture to press it upon your earnest attention. It seems to be very evident that the provision of regular steam postal communication by aid from government has been the forerunner of the commercial predominance of Great Britain on all these coasts and seas, a greater share in whose trade is now the desire and the intent of our people. It is also manifest that the efforts of other European nations to contend with Great Britain for a share of this commerce have been successful in proportion with their adoption of regular steam postal communication with the markets whose trade they sought. Mexico and the States of South America are anxious to receive such postal communication with this country and to aid in their development. Similar cooperation may be looked for in due time from the Eastern nations and from Australia. It is difficult to see how the lead in this movement can be expected from private interests. In respect of foreign commerce quite as much as in internal trade postal communication seems necessarily a matter of common and public administration, and thus pertaining to Government. I respectfully recommend to your prompt attention such just and efficient measures as may conduce to the development of our foreign commercial exchanges and the building up of our carrying trade.

In this connection I desire also to suggest the very great service which might be expected in enlarging and facilitating our commerce on the Pacific Ocean were a transmarine cable laid from San Francisco to the Sandwich Islands, and thence to Japan at the north and Australia at the south. The great influence of such means of communication on these routes of navigation in developing and securing the due share of our Pacific Coast in the commerce of the world needs no illustration or enforcement. It may be that such an enterprise, useful, and in the end profitable, as it would prove to private investment, may need to be accelerated by prudent legislation by Congress in its aid, and I submit the matter to your careful consideration.

An additional and not unimportant, although secondary, reason for fostering and enlarging the Navy may be found in the unquestionable service to the expansion of our commerce which would be rendered by the frequent circulation of naval ships in the seas and ports of all quarters of the globe. Ships of the proper construction and equipment to be of the greatest efficiency in case of maritime war might be made constant and active agents in time of peace in the advancement and protection of our foreign trade and in the nurture and discipline of young seamen, who would naturally in some numbers mix with and improve the crews of our merchant ships. Our merchants at home and abroad recognize the value to foreign commerce of an active movement of our naval vessels, and the intelligence and patriotic zeal of our naval officers in promoting every interest of their countrymen is a just subject of national pride.

The condition of the financial affairs of the Government, as shown by the report of the Secretary of the Treasury, is very satisfactory. It is believed that the present financial situation of the United States, whether considered with respect to trade, currency, credit, growing wealth, or the extent and variety of our resources, is more favorable than that of any other country of our time, and has never been surpassed by that of any country at any period of its history. All our industries are thriving; the rate of interest is low; new railroads are being constructed; a vast immigration is increasing our population, capital, and labor; new enterprises in great number are in progress, and our commercial relations with other countries are improving. The ordinary revenues from all sources for the fiscal year ended June 30,

1880, were—
From customs - $186,522,064.60
From internal revenue - 124,009,373.92
From sales of public lands - 1,016,506.60
From tax on circulation and deposits of national banks - 7,014,971.44
From repayment of interest by Pacific Railway companies - 1,707,367.18
From sinking fund for Pacific Railway companies - 786,621.22
From customs fees, fines, penalties, etc - 1,148,800.16
From fees-consular, letters patent, and lands - 2,337,029.00
From proceeds of sales of Government property - 282,616.50
From profits on coinage, etc - 2,792,186.78
From revenues of the District of Columbia - 1,809,469.70
From miscellaneous sources - 4,099,603.88